SERVERLESS AZURE TRACK TO FUNCTIONS & LOGIC APPS

FIRST EDITION

Preface

Serverless computing is revolutionizing the way developers build and deploy applications, enabling rapid innovation without the overhead of managing infrastructure. As cloud technologies mature, platforms like Microsoft Azure have taken the lead in offering robust, scalable, and developer-friendly serverless solutions.

"Serverless Azure: Fast Track to Functions & Logic Apps" was born out of a desire to simplify the learning curve for newcomers to Azure's serverless ecosystem. Whether you're a developer taking your first steps into cloud-native development, an IT professional seeking automation solutions, or a tech enthusiast curious about modern architectures, this book will serve as your practical guide.

Throughout this book, we'll take a hands-on approach. You'll start by understanding the fundamentals of serverless computing, followed by working directly with Azure Functions, Logic Apps, and a suite of real-time, orchestrated, and automated services. You'll learn how to build, deploy, and scale your apps effectively with best practices, CI/CD pipelines, and security models tailored for serverless environments. We'll explore performance tuning, cost optimization, and even dip into forward-looking innovations like serverless AI.

Chapters are structured progressively. We begin with the essential concepts and tool setup, then delve into function-based development, workflow automation, and event-driven patterns. From there, you'll gain insights into integrating services, handling long-running processes, and establishing DevOps pipelines. We cap off with real-world use cases to solidify your understanding and give you context for applying your knowledge in enterprise scenarios.

As a beginner-focused guide, we emphasize clarity and context, stripping away jargon where possible and reinforcing learning with examples and best practices. If you follow along, by the end of this book, you'll have built several serverless solutions, set up your CI/CD processes, and be prepared to explore deeper paths in Azure's serverless future.

Welcome aboard, and let's get started building on Azure—without the fluff.

Table of Contents

Chapter 1: Introduction to Serverless on Azure

What is Serverless Computing?

Serverless computing is a cloud-native development model that enables developers to build and run applications without managing servers. In a serverless environment, the cloud provider dynamically allocates resources and handles the infrastructure required to run code. Developers focus solely on writing business logic while the cloud handles everything else—from provisioning servers to scaling and patching.

At its core, serverless is about abstraction. It abstracts the complexity of backend infrastructure, allowing you to think in terms of events, triggers, and responses rather than machines, networks, and runtimes. The main components typically include **Functions-as-a-Service (FaaS)** and **Backend-as-a-Service (BaaS)** offerings.

Key Characteristics of Serverless

- **Event-driven execution**: Functions run in response to specific events, such as HTTP requests, timer schedules, or messages in a queue.

- **Micro-billing**: You're charged only for the compute time your code actually uses.

- **Auto-scaling**: Functions automatically scale up or down based on demand.

- **Statelessness**: Serverless functions are stateless by default, making them ephemeral and scalable.

- **Managed infrastructure**: The cloud provider takes full responsibility for managing the underlying hardware, networking, and runtime.

This model reduces operational overhead and allows faster delivery of features. It's particularly well-suited for microservices, APIs, automation scripts, event-driven processing, and lightweight backend tasks.

Serverless vs Traditional Architecture

Let's compare traditional server-based architecture with serverless:

Feature	Traditional Servers	Serverless
Infrastructure Management	Managed by developers	Managed by cloud provider

Scaling	Manual or script-based	Automatic
Billing	Per server/hour	Per execution/millisecond
Deployment Complexity	High (servers, VMs, containers)	Low (code/function deployment)
Idle Resource Usage	Resources consumed when idle	No charges during inactivity
Operational Burden	High	Low

Real-World Analogy

Think of serverless like using a ride-hailing service instead of owning a car. With a traditional server, you're responsible for everything—the car, maintenance, fuel, and parking. With serverless, you summon a ride when you need it, pay only for the trip, and don't worry about the rest.

Common Misconceptions

- **"Serverless means no servers."**
  Not true. There *are* servers involved, but they are completely abstracted away from you.

- **"It's only for small applications."**
  Serverless can scale to support large, complex systems with millions of invocations per day.

- **"It's insecure or unreliable."**
  Azure's serverless services offer enterprise-grade security, fault tolerance, and compliance.

Serverless Execution Model

In Azure, serverless functions are packaged and deployed to a **Function App**. When an event (like an HTTP request) occurs, Azure loads the appropriate function, executes it, and then deallocates the resources once the execution is complete.

A typical function may look like this in JavaScript:

```
module.exports = async function (context, req) {
    context.log('Serverless function triggered');
```

```
const name = req.query.name || (req.body && req.body.name);
const responseMessage = name
    ? `Hello, ${name}.`
    : "Hello! Please provide a name.";

context.res = {
    status: 200,
    body: responseMessage
};
}
```

This function is triggered by an HTTP request. It responds with a greeting using the provided query or body parameter. Note the absence of any server code—it's just the function and its logic.

Azure's Place in the Serverless Ecosystem

Azure offers a rich suite of serverless tools, including:

- **Azure Functions** – Function-as-a-Service, allowing you to run code in response to events.

- **Logic Apps** – Workflow orchestration using a visual designer.

- **Event Grid** – Event routing service for building event-driven architectures.

- **Service Bus** – Enterprise messaging and integration backbone.

- **Durable Functions** – For long-running and stateful workflows.

Together, these tools can power virtually any serverless application, from lightweight automation scripts to robust enterprise solutions.

When to Use Serverless

Serverless is ideal for:

- API backends

- Real-time data processing

- Webhooks and event-driven systems

- Automation of recurring tasks

- Lightweight microservices

- IoT backends

It's particularly beneficial when you need to scale quickly, iterate fast, and reduce time-to-market.

Limitations to Consider

- **Cold Starts**: Initial execution delay if the function hasn't been used recently.

- **Vendor Lock-In**: Heavy reliance on a cloud provider's ecosystem.

- **Debugging Complexity**: Harder to debug due to ephemeral nature.

- **Timeouts**: Most platforms, including Azure, limit how long a single function can run.

Mitigating these drawbacks often involves architecture decisions (e.g., warming strategies, using Durable Functions, adopting observability tools).

Serverless in Enterprise Environments

For large organizations, serverless presents a compelling value proposition:

- **Reduced cost** during off-hours or for sporadic workloads

- **Rapid prototyping** without heavy infrastructure planning

- **Improved developer productivity** through simplified deployment models

However, enterprises must also consider **governance**, **security**, and **compliance**. Fortunately, Azure offers tools like **Managed Identities**, **Azure Policy**, and **Role-Based Access Control (RBAC)** to address these concerns.

Evolving Developer Mindset

Moving to serverless is not just a technical shift; it's a mindset change. Developers must start thinking in terms of **event-driven** architecture, **granular** logic decomposition, and **statelessness**. The payoff? Increased agility, faster iterations, and systems that scale effortlessly.

Summary

Serverless computing is transforming how modern cloud applications are built. By abstracting infrastructure management, Azure's serverless offerings allow developers to focus purely on delivering business value. As this book progresses, you'll build real-world solutions using Azure's powerful serverless stack, learning by doing—from the ground up.

The serverless future is already here. Let's dive in.

Benefits and Use Cases

Serverless computing brings a multitude of advantages to both individual developers and enterprise organizations. By offloading infrastructure management to the cloud provider and allowing for event-driven execution, serverless creates a more agile, cost-effective, and scalable development environment. In this section, we'll explore the key benefits of serverless computing on Azure, followed by a deep dive into a wide array of use cases where serverless solutions excel.

Key Benefits of Serverless on Azure

1. No Infrastructure Management

Perhaps the most obvious benefit is the elimination of server management tasks. There's no need to provision, patch, or maintain servers. Azure abstracts the infrastructure entirely, letting developers focus purely on writing code or designing workflows.

In traditional models, developers often spend hours (or days) setting up environments, ensuring compatibility, handling networking configurations, and dealing with security patches. In serverless, you write a function or design a workflow, deploy it, and let Azure handle the rest.

2. Auto-Scaling and Elasticity

Azure serverless services automatically scale based on demand. If your API endpoint receives 1,000 requests per second, Azure Functions can scale out to handle those requests in parallel. Conversely, if there's no traffic, your function doesn't run, and you incur no cost.

This level of elasticity is particularly valuable for applications with unpredictable or fluctuating traffic patterns—like marketing campaigns, seasonal e-commerce sites, or sensor data pipelines in IoT systems.

3. Pay-per-Use Billing

Serverless follows a consumption-based pricing model. With Azure Functions, you are charged based on the number of executions and the execution duration (in GB-seconds). For Logic Apps, pricing is based on the number of actions or connectors executed.

This model is significantly more cost-effective for applications with intermittent workloads. You are no longer paying for idle resources; you pay only for what you use.

4. Faster Time to Market

Because there's less setup and no infrastructure provisioning, teams can move faster. Developers can prototype new ideas quickly, test them in production-like environments, and deploy changes frequently using modern CI/CD pipelines.

Moreover, serverless encourages a modular, function-based approach to application development. This promotes better code reuse, easier testing, and isolated deployments—enabling faster iteration cycles.

5. Built-in High Availability

Azure Functions and Logic Apps run in highly available and fault-tolerant infrastructure. Azure manages failover, redundancy, and disaster recovery without user intervention.

For mission-critical applications, this built-in availability is a major advantage. You can rely on Azure's global infrastructure to keep your serverless apps running with minimal downtime and resilience against failures.

6. Simplified Event-Driven Development

Azure provides rich integration with events via Event Grid, Service Bus, and Storage Queues. This enables clean and scalable event-driven architectures, where components react to changes asynchronously.

Serverless is inherently suited to event-driven models, whether it's reacting to file uploads, incoming messages, database changes, or webhook events. These scenarios become incredibly simple to implement and extend.

7. Seamless Integration with Azure Ecosystem

Azure serverless services integrate deeply with other Azure resources. You can authenticate with Azure AD, connect securely to databases, automate resource provisioning, and monitor performance—all within a cohesive ecosystem.

This native integration reduces complexity and promotes consistency across your architecture.

Serverless Use Cases

Now that we've seen the benefits, let's look at how those translate into practical, real-world scenarios. Serverless computing shines in dozens of areas across industries and domains. Here, we'll break them down by categories.

1. API Backends

One of the most common uses of serverless is building API backends. Azure Functions can be exposed via HTTP triggers, making them perfect for handling RESTful endpoints.

Example: You could build a full CRUD API for managing user profiles using Azure Functions, Cosmos DB, and Azure API Management for security and throttling.

```
[FunctionName("GetUser")]
public static async Task<IActionResult> Run(
    [HttpTrigger(AuthorizationLevel.Function, "get", Route =
"users/{id}")] HttpRequest req,
    string id,
    ILogger log)
{
    var user = await GetUserFromDatabaseAsync(id);
    return user is null ? new NotFoundResult() : new
OkObjectResult(user);
}
```

Combine this with Logic Apps to send welcome emails, add logging to Application Insights, and trigger workflows for onboarding.

2. Scheduled Tasks and Automation

Serverless is great for automating periodic tasks. This could include:

- Cleaning up old files from a storage container every night

- Sending a daily sales report

- Reindexing a database

These tasks can be implemented using time-based triggers (CRON expressions) in Azure Functions or Recurrence triggers in Logic Apps.

```
"schedule": {
  "frequency": "Day",
  "interval": 1
}
```

3. Real-Time File Processing

When a file is uploaded to Azure Blob Storage, you can trigger a Function to:

- Validate the file format

- Extract metadata

- Move it to another container

- Send a notification to a team

This is common in content pipelines, compliance processing, and digital asset management.

4. Chatbots and Virtual Assistants

Using serverless alongside Azure Bot Services, you can implement custom logic in serverless functions to handle user inputs, call external APIs, store conversations, or trigger workflows.

Chatbots can benefit from:

- Azure Functions for stateless conversations

- Durable Functions for long-running dialogs

- Logic Apps for external system integration

5. Internet of Things (IoT)

IoT devices often generate vast amounts of telemetry. Azure Event Hubs or IoT Hub can stream this data to Azure Functions for real-time processing.

Scenarios include:

- Temperature anomaly detection

- Predictive maintenance

- Real-time dashboards and alerts

With serverless, you avoid having a dedicated processing pipeline running 24/7. You process data as it arrives.

6. E-commerce and Marketing Automation

E-commerce businesses can automate:

- Cart abandonment emails

- Promotional notifications

- Order confirmation workflows

- Inventory updates from supplier APIs

Logic Apps excel here because they can visually orchestrate email, CRM, and payment systems without code, and Azure Functions handle the custom logic.

7. Image and Video Processing

Azure Functions can be used to automatically process uploaded media. For example:

- Generate thumbnails for images

- Transcode video files

- Detect objects or faces using Cognitive Services

This event-driven processing model scales with demand and avoids over-provisioning resources.

8. Data Pipelines and ETL Jobs

Serverless simplifies Extract, Transform, Load (ETL) processes. You can:

- Trigger a function when new data arrives in a database

- Normalize or clean the data

- Store it in a data warehouse or Cosmos DB

- Trigger Power BI dashboard updates

This pattern supports both batch and streaming models.

9. Financial and Legal Workflows

Industries like finance and law benefit from serverless automation for:

- Document classification and OCR

- Automated compliance workflows

- Secure notification systems

Serverless is often combined with Azure Key Vault and Managed Identities for high levels of security.

10. Education and Research

In educational apps, you can automate:

- Assignment reminders

- Grading summaries

- Student engagement tracking

- Content publishing workflows

Serverless allows small development teams to launch powerful education tools quickly without infrastructure headaches.

Combining Serverless Components for Maximum Impact

The real power of Azure serverless solutions lies in combining services like Functions, Logic Apps, Event Grid, and Cosmos DB into cohesive, event-driven systems.

Example Architecture:

- A Logic App receives a webhook from a third-party form submission.

- It triggers an Azure Function that validates and transforms the data.

- The function stores the data in a Cosmos DB collection.

- Event Grid fires an event when the data is inserted.

- A second function listens to the event and sends a real-time email notification.

- Application Insights tracks execution and performance.

This kind of loosely coupled architecture is:

- Easier to scale

- Easier to maintain

- More resilient to failures

- Highly modular and testable

Summary

Serverless computing enables agile, scalable, and cost-effective development. By removing the burden of infrastructure and embracing an event-driven model, Azure serverless services empower teams to build powerful applications faster and more efficiently.

Whether you're building an API, automating workflows, handling real-time data, or running periodic jobs, serverless offers a compelling path forward. As cloud adoption grows and digital transformation accelerates, serverless will continue to play a pivotal role across industries.

The next chapter will guide you through Azure Functions—the core building block of serverless development on Azure—so you can begin building your own powerful applications.

A network error occurred. Please check your connection and try again. If this issue persists please contact us through our help center at help.openai.com.

Azure's Serverless Suite Overview

Azure offers a rich ecosystem of serverless services designed to accommodate a wide variety of application needs, ranging from simple automation to enterprise-scale solutions. These services span compute, workflow orchestration, messaging, monitoring, and security, forming a cohesive platform for building event-driven, scalable, and cost-efficient applications.

In this section, we'll explore the core components of Azure's serverless suite. Each service brings its own strengths and is best suited for specific scenarios, but together, they empower developers to architect sophisticated, integrated solutions.

Core Serverless Services

Azure Functions

Azure Functions is Microsoft's Function-as-a-Service (FaaS) offering. It allows you to run small pieces of code (functions) in response to a variety of events. Functions are stateless, triggered on-demand, and automatically scaled.

Key Features:

- Supports multiple languages: C#, JavaScript, TypeScript, Python, Java, PowerShell, etc.

- Event-driven: supports HTTP, timer, queue, blob, Event Hub, and more as triggers.

- Auto-scaling: functions scale out automatically based on demand.

- Durable Functions: extension for orchestrating long-running workflows.

- Integrates with Application Insights for monitoring and logging.

Example Use Case:

Trigger a function every time a user uploads a file to Blob Storage, analyze the file content, and store the results in Cosmos DB.

```
[FunctionName("BlobTriggerFunction")]
public static void Run(
    [BlobTrigger("uploads/{name}", Connection =
"AzureWebJobsStorage")] Stream myBlob,
    string name,
    ILogger log)
{
    log.LogInformation($"Blob trigger function processed blob\n
Name:{name} \n Size: {myBlob.Length} Bytes");
}
```

Logic Apps

Azure Logic Apps provide a no-code/low-code workflow automation platform. Using a visual designer or JSON-based definitions, you can automate processes by chaining together triggers, actions, and conditions.

Key Features:

- Connects to over 600 built-in and third-party connectors (e.g., SharePoint, Salesforce, Twitter, SQL Server).

- Supports looping, branching, conditions, and error handling.

- Ideal for integrating systems and orchestrating business processes.

- Can call Azure Functions for custom logic.

- Supports stateful and stateless executions.

Example Use Case:

Create a Logic App that triggers when an email is received with an attachment, stores the attachment in OneDrive, and sends a Teams notification.

Event Grid

Azure Event Grid is an event routing service that enables reactive programming. It allows you to publish and subscribe to events across Azure services or custom applications.

Key Features:

- Built for high-throughput, low-latency event delivery.

- Supports native Azure services as event sources (e.g., Blob Storage, Resource Groups).

- Enables custom topics and custom event sources.

- Delivers events to endpoints like Azure Functions, Logic Apps, Event Hubs, and Webhooks.

Example Use Case:

When a blob is created in a storage container, Event Grid sends an event to an Azure Function, which processes the file.

Service Bus

Azure Service Bus is a fully managed enterprise message broker. It supports advanced messaging features, making it ideal for decoupling components of a distributed system.

Key Features:

- Supports queues and publish-subscribe topics.

- Ensures reliable message delivery with dead-letter queues and retries.

- Supports FIFO, session-based messaging, and duplicate detection.

- Integrates with Functions and Logic Apps as a trigger or action.

Example Use Case:

An order-processing application uses Service Bus to queue incoming orders. A Function app reads from the queue, validates the orders, and updates a database.

Queue Storage

Azure Queue Storage is a simple message queueing service for basic workloads.

Key Features:

- Ideal for basic message processing pipelines.

- Trigger Azure Functions when a new message is added.

- Simple, cost-effective, and easy to integrate.

Example Use Case:

Send user-generated content moderation requests to a queue. A function processes messages one by one, applying filters and rules.

Complementary Services

To build fully operational and production-ready serverless applications, Azure provides several supporting services:

Azure Key Vault

Used to store and access secrets, keys, and certificates securely. Functions and Logic Apps can retrieve secrets at runtime using Managed Identities.

Benefits:

- Secure, centralized storage for sensitive configuration.

- RBAC and policy enforcement.

- Integration with .NET, JavaScript, and Python SDKs.

Example:

An Azure Function retrieving an API key stored in Key Vault:

```
var kvClient = new SecretClient(new Uri(keyVaultUri), new
DefaultAzureCredential());
KeyVaultSecret secret = await kvClient.GetSecretAsync("MyApiKey");
string apiKey = secret.Value;
```

Application Insights

Provides logging, tracing, and telemetry for monitoring serverless applications.

Capabilities:

- Track custom events, exceptions, and dependencies.

- Analyze cold starts and performance bottlenecks.

- Real-time dashboards and query support with Kusto Query Language (KQL).

Example:

Log a custom trace in an Azure Function:

```
log.LogInformation("Order processed successfully for OrderID:
12345");
```

Azure Monitor

A comprehensive monitoring solution that includes metrics, logs, alerts, and dashboards. Works with Application Insights to provide a full picture of system health.

Use Azure Monitor to:

- Set up alerts for failed function executions.

- Monitor Logic App runs and trigger failures.

- Visualize function throughput and performance trends.

Orchestration Scenarios

Serverless applications often require combining multiple components to form larger workflows. Azure supports orchestration in various ways:

Using Durable Functions

Durable Functions extend Azure Functions with capabilities like:

- Chaining: Run functions in sequence.

- Fan-out/fan-in: Run multiple functions in parallel and aggregate results.

- Waiting for external events: Useful for approval workflows.

- Sub-orchestrations: Build modular, reusable workflows.

Example:

Orchestrate a travel booking process:

1. Book flight

2. Book hotel

3. Reserve car

4. Send confirmation email

```
[FunctionName("TravelBookingOrchestrator")]
public static async Task<List<string>> RunOrchestrator(
    [OrchestrationTrigger] IDurableOrchestrationContext context)
{
    var outputs = new List<string>();

    outputs.Add(await
context.CallActivityAsync<string>("BookFlight", null));
    outputs.Add(await context.CallActivityAsync<string>("BookHotel",
null));
    outputs.Add(await
context.CallActivityAsync<string>("ReserveCar", null));

    return outputs;
}
```

Using Logic Apps for Orchestration

Logic Apps are great for long-running workflows that involve external systems and human input. With built-in connectors and conditional logic, they make building orchestrations easy and visual.

Example Use Case:

A HR onboarding workflow:

- Starts with a SharePoint form submission.

- Sends approval request to a manager via Outlook.

- Creates user in Azure AD.

- Sends welcome package via email.

Choosing the Right Serverless Tool

Each component in the Azure serverless suite is optimized for specific scenarios. Here's a quick comparison to help you choose the right tool for your use case:

Scenario	Recommended Tool
Stateless backend logic	Azure Functions
Workflow automation	Logic Apps
Complex orchestrations	Durable Functions
Messaging between services	Service Bus
Event-based reactions	Event Grid
Lightweight queues	Queue Storage
Secrets management	Azure Key Vault
Observability and logs	Application Insights, Azure Monitor

Integration Across Services

In most real-world applications, you won't rely on a single serverless service. The true strength of Azure's serverless ecosystem lies in its integration capabilities.

Integrated Example:

- Event Grid receives a Blob Storage event.

- Event triggers an Azure Function.

- Function queries Cosmos DB and enriches the event data.

- Enriched data is posted to a Logic App.

- Logic App sends the data to a CRM system and notifies a Slack channel.

- All activity is monitored via Application Insights.

This tight integration between services supports composability, flexibility, and maintainability.

Summary

Azure's serverless suite is a robust, enterprise-grade platform designed to support a wide range of application needs—from simple automation tasks to complex, orchestrated business processes. With services like Azure Functions, Logic Apps, Event Grid, and Service Bus at your disposal, you can build reactive, cost-efficient systems that scale effortlessly.

Each component in the suite serves a specific role, and when combined, they enable powerful solutions that are event-driven, resilient, and easy to maintain. As we progress through this book, you'll get hands-on experience with these tools, learning how to integrate them into full-fledged applications that solve real-world problems.

Prerequisites and Tools Setup

Before you dive into building serverless applications on Azure, it's essential to have a well-prepared development environment. Azure's serverless platform is designed to be developer-friendly and offers a wide range of tools that integrate seamlessly into various operating systems, IDEs, and CI/CD pipelines. In this section, we'll walk through the setup process step-by-step and explain the essential tools, SDKs, and configurations you need to get started.

We'll cover:

- Azure account setup

- Required tools and SDKs

- Azure CLI and Azure PowerShell

- Visual Studio Code setup

- Function Core Tools installation

- Logic Apps designer setup

- Creating your first Azure project locally

- Resource group and storage setup

- Best practices for development environments

Creating an Azure Account

To start building with Azure, you need a Microsoft Azure account. If you don't have one, you can sign up at:

https://azure.microsoft.com/en-us/free

Azure provides a generous **free tier** that includes monthly usage of Azure Functions, Logic Apps, Event Grid, and more—ideal for development and testing.

After creating your account:

1. Log into the Azure Portal.

2. Navigate to the **Subscription** page and verify you're using the correct subscription tier.

3. Optionally, enable multi-factor authentication for added security.

Installing the Azure CLI

The **Azure Command-Line Interface (CLI)** is a cross-platform command-line tool that allows you to manage Azure resources directly from your terminal. It's one of the most essential tools in the Azure development toolkit.

Installation

Install the CLI using the appropriate command for your OS:

Windows:

```
Invoke-WebRequest -Uri https://aka.ms/installazurecliwindows -
OutFile .\AzureCLI.msi; Start-Process msiexec.exe -Wait -
ArgumentList '/I AzureCLI.msi /quiet'
```

macOS (Homebrew):

```
brew update && brew install azure-cli
```

Linux (Debian-based):

```
curl -sL https://aka.ms/InstallAzureCLIDeb | sudo bash
```

Verify Installation

Run the following command to confirm successful installation:

```
az --version
```

Login and Configuration

To log in:

```
az login
```

This opens a browser window to authenticate your session. If you're using a service principal for automation:

```
az login --service-principal --username <APP_ID> --password
<PASSWORD> --tenant <TENANT_ID>
```

Installing Azure PowerShell (Optional)

If you prefer PowerShell or are automating using Azure scripts in Windows environments, install the Azure PowerShell module.

```
Install-Module -Name Az -Scope CurrentUser -Repository PSGallery -
Force
```

To sign in:

```
Connect-AzAccount
```

Installing Visual Studio Code

Visual Studio Code (VS Code) is the recommended IDE for serverless development. It supports Azure Functions and Logic Apps extensions and provides rich integration with debugging, IntelliSense, and Git.

1. Download and install from https://code.visualstudio.com.

2. Install the following extensions from the Extensions marketplace:

   - **Azure Tools**

   - **Azure Functions**

   - **Azure Account**

   - **C#** (if using C#)

   - **Python** (if using Python)

   - **Docker** (if using containers)

Installing Azure Functions Core Tools

Azure Functions Core Tools enable you to create, run, and debug serverless functions locally before deploying them to Azure.

Installation

macOS (Homebrew):

```
brew tap azure/functions
brew install azure-functions-core-tools@4
```

Windows (npm):

```
npm i -g azure-functions-core-tools@4 --unsafe-perm true
```

Linux: Refer to https://docs.microsoft.com/azure/azure-functions/functions-run-local for specific package manager instructions.

Verify Installation
```
func --version
```

You should see output like: `4.x.x`

Setting Up the Logic Apps Designer

Logic Apps can be created directly from the Azure Portal or locally using Visual Studio Code.

To use the **Logic Apps Standard** (which runs locally and supports CI/CD):

1. Install **Azure Logic Apps (Standard) extension** in VS Code.

Install **Azure Logic Apps Tools** globally:

```
npm install -g @microsoft/logic-apps-cli
```

2.

Initialize a new project:

```
mkdir MyLogicApp && cd MyLogicApp
logicapp init
```

3.
4. Use the graphical designer in VS Code to create workflows.

5. Deploy using Azure CLI or directly through VS Code.

Creating a Local Function Project

Let's walk through setting up a function project locally.

```
func init MyFunctionApp --worker-runtime dotnet
cd MyFunctionApp
func new --name HelloWorld --template "HTTP trigger" --authlevel
"anonymous"
```

This generates a basic HTTP-triggered function. You can test it locally:

```
func start
```

You'll see a local endpoint like:

```
http://localhost:7071/api/HelloWorld
```

Try it in your browser or via curl:

```
curl http://localhost:7071/api/HelloWorld?name=Azure
```

Creating Resource Groups and Storage Accounts

Azure Functions require a **Storage Account** to persist metadata. Before deploying your functions, create a resource group and a storage account:

```
az group create --name myResourceGroup --location westeurope

az storage account create \
  --name mystorageaccountname \
  --location westeurope \
  --resource-group myResourceGroup \
  --sku Standard_LRS
```

You can then deploy your Function App:

```
az functionapp create \
  --resource-group myResourceGroup \
  --consumption-plan-location westeurope \
  --runtime dotnet \
  --functions-version 4 \
  --name myFunctionAppName \
  --storage-account mystorageaccountname
```

Setting Up Git and GitHub Integration

Azure integrates smoothly with GitHub for source control and CI/CD. If you haven't already:

1. Install Git: https://git-scm.com

Initialize your project:

```
git init
git remote add origin https://github.com/your-username/your-repo.git
git add .
```

```
git commit -m "Initial commit"
git push -u origin main
```

2.
3. Set up **GitHub Actions** or Azure DevOps pipelines for automatic deployments.

Optional: Installing Docker

While not strictly required, Docker is useful for packaging Functions or Logic Apps into containers. To install:

macOS and Windows: https://www.docker.com/products/docker-desktop

Use Docker to run functions in containerized environments:

```
func init --docker
docker build -t myfunctionapp .
docker run -p 8080:80 myfunctionapp
```

Recommended Best Practices

- **Use Environment Variables:** Store configuration values using `local.settings.json` locally and App Settings in Azure.

- **Leverage Managed Identities:** Use identities instead of hardcoded secrets for accessing other Azure resources.

- **Automate Setup:** Use Bicep or ARM templates to script resource provisioning.

- **Secure Access:** Use Azure Key Vault and RBAC policies.

- **Debug Locally First:** Use Core Tools and Application Insights to troubleshoot before deployment.

- **Adopt CI/CD Early:** Set up GitHub Actions or Azure Pipelines to deploy with consistency.

- **Tag Resources:** Apply naming conventions and metadata to keep your environment organized.

Summary

With your development environment configured, you're now ready to build and deploy serverless applications on Azure. You've installed critical tools like the Azure CLI, Function Core Tools, and VS Code, and configured your system to develop both Azure Functions and Logic Apps locally. You've also set up the Azure environment—subscription, resource groups, and storage—ensuring you can deploy without manual configuration later.

In the chapters that follow, you'll begin to build real solutions using this setup. As you work through examples, you'll rely on the tools and practices outlined here to develop, debug, and deploy confidently in a real-world Azure serverless environment.

Chapter 2: Azure Functions: The Building Blocks

Understanding Azure Functions Architecture

Azure Functions represent one of the most prominent examples of serverless computing within the Azure ecosystem. They allow developers to focus on the logic that matters most while Azure handles the infrastructure, scaling, and execution. Understanding the architecture of Azure Functions is critical to building efficient, scalable, and maintainable applications.

This section provides a comprehensive breakdown of how Azure Functions work, including their underlying components, hosting plans, execution lifecycle, triggers and bindings model, state management options, scaling mechanics, deployment considerations, and architectural best practices.

What Are Azure Functions?

Azure Functions are a compute-on-demand service that lets you run event-driven code without explicitly provisioning or managing servers. Each function is triggered by an event, such as an HTTP request, a message arriving in a queue, or a timer. They are the building blocks of microservices in serverless architectures.

Functions are organized into **Function Apps**, which act as the deployment and management unit. Within a Function App, you can group multiple functions that share configuration, runtime versions, and scaling rules.

Function App Architecture

A **Function App** is the container for one or more individual functions and includes:

- **Runtime environment** (e.g., .NET, Node.js, Python, Java)

- **Shared configuration** (App Settings, storage accounts, etc.)

- **Deployment credentials and versioning**

- **Hosting plan and scaling policy**

- **Bindings and extensions configuration**

Functions inside the same Function App run in the same environment and can share resources like files or memory.

Execution Lifecycle

The lifecycle of a function execution in Azure consists of the following stages:

1. **Trigger Activation**: An event (e.g., HTTP request, queue message) occurs.

2. **Instance Allocation**: Azure spins up a compute instance if needed.

3. **Function Execution**: The user-defined code is executed.

4. **Output Binding Execution**: The output is routed to the configured binding (e.g., database, blob).

5. **Logging & Metrics**: Execution telemetry is sent to Application Insights or Azure Monitor.

6. **Teardown (If Idle)**: The instance may be deallocated if idle, depending on the hosting plan.

Triggers and Bindings Model

Triggers and bindings are a unique feature of Azure Functions, allowing integration with various services in a declarative way.

Trigger

A **trigger** defines how a function is invoked. Only one trigger is allowed per function.

Examples:

- HTTP Trigger

- Timer Trigger

- Blob Trigger

- Queue Trigger

- Event Hub Trigger

Input and Output Bindings

Bindings allow data to flow into and out of the function without writing boilerplate code to connect services.

Input Binding example:

```
{
  "name": "myBlob",
  "type": "blob",
  "direction": "in",
  "path": "samples-workitems/{name}",
  "connection": "AzureWebJobsStorage"
}
```

Output Binding example:

```
{
  "name": "outputQueueItem",
  "type": "queue",
  "direction": "out",
  "queueName": "processed-items",
  "connection": "AzureWebJobsStorage"
}
```

These bindings are configured in the `function.json` file or via annotations in supported languages.

Hosting Plans

Azure Functions can run under three main hosting plans:

1. Consumption Plan

- Auto-scales based on demand.

- Billed per execution and resource consumption.

- Cold start delays possible.

- Default plan for event-driven and lightweight workloads.

2. Premium Plan

- Pre-warmed instances to avoid cold starts.

- More powerful VM options.

- Supports VNET integration and unlimited execution duration.

- Ideal for production-critical workloads.

3. Dedicated (App Service) Plan

- Functions run on dedicated VMs.

- Shares resources with other App Services.

- Useful for scenarios where other App Services already exist and need integration.

Each hosting plan supports different scaling and billing characteristics, so choosing the right plan is essential for performance and cost management.

Scaling Model

Azure Functions scale based on the number of incoming events and the nature of the trigger. The scale controller (a part of the Azure infrastructure) monitors event sources and adjusts the number of function instances accordingly.

Examples:

- **HTTP Trigger**: Scales based on HTTP request volume.

- **Queue Trigger**: Scales based on queue length and dequeue rate.

- **Event Hub Trigger**: Scales based on the number of partitions.

Scaling is transparent to the developer but can be influenced by limits in the hosting plan or code-level constraints (e.g., concurrency).

Runtime and Languages

Azure Functions supports multiple runtime versions and programming languages:

- .NET Core / .NET 6+

- JavaScript / TypeScript

- Python

- Java

- PowerShell

- Custom Handlers (for any language using HTTP-in/HTTP-out protocol)

Choosing the right language depends on team skillsets, ecosystem support, and performance requirements. .NET and JavaScript are the most mature runtimes in Azure Functions.

Local Development and Debugging

Developers can write and test Azure Functions locally using:

- **Azure Functions Core Tools**

- **Visual Studio or Visual Studio Code**

- **Local emulators for bindings** (e.g., Azure Storage Emulator or Azurite)

Example using Core Tools:

```
func init MyFunctionApp --worker-runtime dotnet
cd MyFunctionApp
func new --name ProcessOrder --template "Queue trigger"
func start
```

This starts a local runtime that mimics the Azure environment, allowing full debugging and inspection.

Durable Functions

Durable Functions is an extension of Azure Functions that adds **stateful workflows** to serverless applications. It enables complex patterns like:

- Function chaining

- Fan-out/fan-in

- Waiting for external events

- Human interaction

Durable Functions uses an **orchestration function** to coordinate activities. State is automatically persisted between steps using Azure Storage.

Example:

```
[FunctionName("MyOrchestrator")]
public static async Task RunOrchestrator(
    [OrchestrationTrigger] IDurableOrchestrationContext context)
{
    var result1 = await context.CallActivityAsync<string>("StepOne",
null);
    var result2 = await context.CallActivityAsync<string>("StepTwo",
result1);
    return result2;
}
```

Durable Functions are ideal for long-running processes such as approval flows, batch jobs, and ETL pipelines.

Integration with Other Services

Azure Functions can easily integrate with:

- **Azure Logic Apps**: Offload workflow orchestration.

- **Azure API Management**: Secure and expose APIs built with Functions.

- **Azure Cosmos DB**: Store and retrieve JSON documents at scale.

- **Azure Event Grid / Service Bus**: Drive event-based architectures.

- **Azure Key Vault**: Securely manage secrets and credentials.

These integrations are facilitated via bindings or programmatic SDKs.

Security and Identity

Security is critical in serverless apps. Azure Functions supports:

- **Managed Identities**: Securely authenticate with Azure services without secrets.

- **Role-Based Access Control (RBAC)**: Restrict access to functions and underlying resources.

- **Network Isolation**: Using VNET integration (Premium Plan only).

- **Authentication Providers**: Built-in support for Azure AD, Facebook, Google, and Twitter.

Use the `identity` block in your `functionapp` deployment for enabling managed identity:

```
az functionapp identity assign --name myFuncApp --resource-group
myResourceGroup
```

Logging and Monitoring

Functions are automatically monitored through:

- **Application Insights**: Collects traces, metrics, requests, exceptions.

- **Azure Monitor**: For system-level metrics and alerts.

- **Live Metrics Stream**: View live requests and performance during development.

Example of a custom log entry:

```
log.LogInformation("Payment processing started at: {time}",
DateTime.Now);
```

Use **Kusto Query Language (KQL)** in Azure Monitor Logs to analyze telemetry:

```
requests
| where cloud_RoleName == "myfunctionapp"
| summarize count() by bin(timestamp, 1h)
```

Deployment Options

Azure Functions support several deployment methods:

- **Visual Studio/VS Code**

- **Azure CLI (`az functionapp deploy`)**

- **GitHub Actions**

- **Azure DevOps Pipelines**

- **ZIP Deploy and FTP**

Choose your deployment method based on your team workflow. For automation and CI/CD, GitHub Actions are a preferred option.

GitHub Actions example:

```
- name: Deploy to Azure Function App
  uses: Azure/functions-action@v1
  with:
    app-name: 'my-function-app'
    package: '.'
```

Best Practices

- Keep functions **small and focused**.

- Use **async** programming to improve performance.

- Avoid blocking calls or long startup tasks.

- **Separate business logic** from function code for testability.

- Use **Dependency Injection** in .NET Functions for better structure.

- Log **meaningful** messages at appropriate log levels.

- **Version** your APIs and use Azure API Management when exposing public endpoints.

- **Protect secrets** using Azure Key Vault.

- Monitor performance using **Application Insights**.

Summary

Understanding the architecture of Azure Functions is foundational to building effective serverless applications. From execution lifecycle and triggers to bindings, hosting plans, and scaling mechanics, every element contributes to how your application behaves and performs.

As you move forward, the concepts covered in this section will guide how you structure your functions, integrate with other Azure services, and make critical design decisions. Azure Functions are flexible, powerful, and production-ready—perfect for building cloud-native apps that are scalable, maintainable, and fast to deploy.

Creating Your First Function App

Creating your first Azure Function App is an essential step in understanding how serverless development works within the Azure ecosystem. This section walks through the entire lifecycle of creating, running, and deploying your first function—from setting up the project locally to pushing it to the cloud. You will explore key concepts such as triggers, bindings, local development, deployment models, and basic testing.

Setting Up Your Local Environment

Before writing code, ensure your environment is ready with the following prerequisites:

- **Azure CLI** installed (az)

- **Azure Functions Core Tools** installed (func)

- **Visual Studio Code** (or another IDE)

- **Azure Subscription** with an active account

- **Azure Storage Account** for deployment

To verify installations:

```
az --version
func --version
```

Both commands should return version numbers indicating successful setup.

Step 1: Initialize the Function App Project

Start by creating a local folder for your project and initializing it with the desired runtime.

```
mkdir HelloFunctionApp
cd HelloFunctionApp
func init --worker-runtime dotnet
```

The `--worker-runtime` can be `dotnet`, `node`, `python`, `java`, or `powershell`. For this example, we'll use C# with `.NET`.

You'll see the following structure created:

```
HelloFunctionApp/
├── host.json
└── local.settings.json
```

- `host.json`: global configuration file for the Function App

- `local.settings.json`: local config including connection strings and environment variables

---

Step 2: Create Your First Function

To create a function:

```
func new
```

You'll be prompted to select a template. Choose:

```
HTTP trigger
```

Provide a name, e.g., `HelloFunction`, and choose the authorization level (e.g., `Anonymous` for simplicity).

This adds a new directory:

```
HelloFunctionApp/
├── HelloFunction/
│   ├── function.json
│   └── run.csx or .cs file
```

For .NET, the file `HelloFunction.cs` might look like:

```csharp
public static class HelloFunction
{
    [FunctionName("HelloFunction")]
    public static IActionResult Run(
        [HttpTrigger(AuthorizationLevel.Anonymous, "get", "post",
Route = null)] HttpRequest req,
        ILogger log)
    {
        log.LogInformation("C# HTTP trigger function processed a
request.");

        string name = req.Query["name"];
        return name != null
            ? (ActionResult)new OkObjectResult($"Hello, {name}")
            : new BadRequestObjectResult("Please pass a name on the
query string");
    }
}
```

This function accepts HTTP GET or POST requests, checks for a query parameter called name, and responds with a greeting.

Step 3: Run and Test Locally

Use the Core Tools to run the Function App locally:

```
func start
```

You'll see output like:

```
Http Functions:
    HelloFunction: http://localhost:7071/api/HelloFunction
```

Test it with a browser or curl:

```
curl http://localhost:7071/api/HelloFunction?name=Azure
```

Expected response:

```
Hello, Azure
```

Logs will show up in the terminal, indicating successful execution and duration.

Step 4: Review Configuration Files

`function.json`

Each function includes a `function.json` file that describes the bindings:

```
{
  "bindings": [
    {
      "authLevel": "anonymous",
      "type": "httpTrigger",
      "direction": "in",
      "name": "req",
      "methods": ["get", "post"]
    },
    {
      "type": "http",
      "direction": "out",
      "name": "$return"
    }
  ]
}
```

This tells Azure how the function is triggered (HTTP) and how it responds (HTTP output).

`local.settings.json`

Stores local settings:

```
{
```

```
  "IsEncrypted": false,
  "Values": {
    "AzureWebJobsStorage": "UseDevelopmentStorage=true",
    "FUNCTIONS_WORKER_RUNTIME": "dotnet"
  }
}
```

Do not commit this file to source control if it includes secrets or keys.

Step 5: Create Required Azure Resources

You need a **Resource Group**, **Storage Account**, and **Function App** in Azure.

```
az group create --name myResourceGroup --location westeurope

az storage account create \
  --name mystorageacct \
  --location westeurope \
  --resource-group myResourceGroup \
  --sku Standard_LRS

az functionapp create \
  --name hello-function-app-001 \
  --resource-group myResourceGroup \
  --storage-account mystorageacct \
  --consumption-plan-location westeurope \
  --runtime dotnet \
  --functions-version 4
```

Step 6: Deploy to Azure

Once your Azure resources are ready, deploy using:

```
func azure functionapp publish hello-function-app-001
```

Deployment output will include:

- URL for your deployed function

- Status of deployment

- Any relevant errors

Test the deployed function:

```
curl https://hello-function-app-
001.azurewebsites.net/api/HelloFunction?name=Azure
```

Step 7: Monitor with Application Insights

If Application Insights is enabled, telemetry data from each invocation is available in the Azure Portal under the "Monitor" tab of the Function App.

Common data includes:

- Execution time

- Invocation count

- Success/failure rate

- Custom logs from `ILogger`

Step 8: Modify and Redeploy

Let's update our greeting message:

```
return name != null
    ? (ActionResult)new OkObjectResult($"Welcome to Azure Functions,
{name}!")
    : new BadRequestObjectResult("Please pass a name on the query
string");
```

Rebuild and redeploy:

```
dotnet build
func azure functionapp publish hello-function-app-001
```

New invocations will reflect your changes immediately.

Step 9: Enable CORS (If Needed)

If your function is called from a browser, enable CORS:

```
az functionapp cors add \
  --name hello-function-app-001 \
  --resource-group myResourceGroup \
  --allowed-origins https://yourfrontend.com
```

Step 10: Cleanup Resources (Optional)

To avoid incurring charges:

```
az group delete --name myResourceGroup --yes --no-wait
```

Troubleshooting Tips

- **Cold starts** in the Consumption Plan can delay first executions.

- Ensure you're using a globally unique name for the Function App.

- Check your bindings in `function.json` for typos.

- Use `func diagnostics` for local debugging.

- Check the **Kudu Console** at `https://<app>.scm.azurewebsites.net` for logs and advanced debugging.

Summary

In this section, you created your first Function App from scratch using Azure Functions Core Tools and the Azure CLI. You learned how to:

- Initialize a function project locally

- Create and configure a function

- Run and test locally

- Deploy to Azure

- Monitor and log usage

- Secure and manage your deployment

This workflow establishes a strong foundation for developing more complex serverless applications. In upcoming sections, you'll expand this function with different trigger types, bindings, and integration patterns to build real-world solutions.

Triggers and Bindings Deep Dive

Triggers and bindings are core to the Azure Functions model, enabling seamless integration with a vast range of Azure services and external systems. They form the input/output glue that allows functions to interact with the world around them. By abstracting complex service integrations into declarative configurations, triggers and bindings dramatically simplify the development experience and reduce boilerplate code.

This section takes an in-depth look at how triggers and bindings work, the available types, real-world use cases, and advanced patterns. You'll also learn about configuration practices, limitations, testing strategies, and best practices for building maintainable, production-ready function-based applications.

Understanding Triggers

A **trigger** is what causes a function to execute. Each function must have exactly one trigger. The trigger defines the function's entry point, specifies the data payload, and provides contextual metadata.

Triggers can be broadly categorized into:

- **HTTP-based** (e.g., REST APIs)

- **Timer-based** (e.g., scheduled jobs)

- **Data-based** (e.g., blob, queue, or database changes)

- **Event-based** (e.g., Event Grid, Event Hub, Service Bus)

- **Custom triggers** (via extensions or custom handlers)

Anatomy of a Trigger

Triggers are defined through attributes (in languages like C#) or `function.json` configuration. A basic HTTP trigger looks like this in C#:

```
[FunctionName("HttpExample")]
public static async Task<IActionResult> Run(
    [HttpTrigger(AuthorizationLevel.Function, "get", "post", Route =
null)] HttpRequest req,
    ILogger log)
{
    log.LogInformation("HTTP trigger function received a request.");
    string name = req.Query["name"];
    return new OkObjectResult($"Hello, {name}");
}
```

Here, `[HttpTrigger]` tells Azure the function is invoked via HTTP, and the route is auto-generated from the function name unless specified otherwise.

Common Trigger Types

1. HTTP Trigger

Used for building APIs or webhooks.

- Supports GET, POST, PUT, DELETE, etc.

- Can return any HTTP response.

- Supports route templates.

Example:

```
[HttpTrigger(AuthorizationLevel.Anonymous, "get", Route =
"products/{id}")]
```

Best used for:

- API backends

- Webhooks

- Client-server communication

2. Timer Trigger

Executes on a schedule using CRON expressions.

```
[TimerTrigger("0 */5 * * * *")] // every 5 minutes
```

Useful for:

- Periodic cleanups

- Data backups

- Scheduled reporting

3. Blob Trigger

Triggers when a new blob is added to a storage container.

```
[BlobTrigger("images/{name}", Connection = "AzureWebJobsStorage")]
Stream myBlob
```

Perfect for:

- Media processing

- Ingestion pipelines

- File validation workflows

4. Queue Trigger

Activated when a message arrives in a storage queue.

```
[QueueTrigger("orders", Connection = "AzureWebJobsStorage")]
string orderMessage
```

Use for:

- Asynchronous task processing

- Decoupling services

- Throttling workloads

5. Service Bus Trigger

Supports queues and topics (pub-sub model).

```
[ServiceBusTrigger("orders", Connection = "ServiceBusConnection")]
string message
```

Great for:

- Enterprise-grade messaging

- Guaranteed delivery

- Message routing with topics

6. Event Grid Trigger

Listens for events from Azure services or custom event publishers.

```
[EventGridTrigger]
EventGridEvent eventGridEvent
```

Scenarios:

- Real-time notification systems

- Event-driven microservices

- Serverless integrations with external systems

7. Event Hub Trigger

Processes streaming data from Event Hubs.

```
[EventHubTrigger("iothub", Connection = "EventHubConnection")]
string[] events
```

Best for:

- IoT ingestion

- Telemetry processing

- Real-time analytics

Input and Output Bindings

While triggers define *how* a function starts, **bindings** define *how* it interacts with other data sources.

You can have multiple **input** and **output** bindings, making it easy to read from or write to services without needing SDKs or boilerplate code.

Input Binding Example (Read from Blob)

```
[Blob("mycontainer/sample.txt", FileAccess.Read)]
string blobContents
```

Output Binding Example (Write to Queue)

```
[Queue("processed-orders", Connection = "AzureWebJobsStorage")]
out string outputQueueItem
```

Common Binding Types

Input Bindings

- Azure Blob Storage

- Azure Queue Storage

- Cosmos DB

- SignalR Service

- HTTP (contextual input)

- Table Storage

- SQL Database

Output Bindings

- Azure Blob Storage

- Azure Queue Storage

- Azure Table Storage

- Cosmos DB

- SignalR

- Event Hubs

- Service Bus

- SendGrid (email)

Example: Function with Input and Output Bindings

Let's create a function that reads a file from Blob Storage and queues a message with its metadata:

```
[FunctionName("ProcessBlob")]
public static void Run(
    [BlobTrigger("uploads/{name}", Connection =
"AzureWebJobsStorage")] Stream blobStream,
    string name,
    [Queue("metadata-queue", Connection = "AzureWebJobsStorage")]
out string queueMessage,
    ILogger log)
{
    log.LogInformation($"Processing blob: {name}");
    queueMessage = $"File {name} of size {blobStream.Length} bytes
processed.";
}
```

No SDKs, no serialization code—just focus on logic.

Binding Expressions

Binding paths can include **binding expressions**, which are resolved from trigger data.

Example:

```
[Blob("backups/{name}", FileAccess.Write)]
```

Here, {name} comes from the trigger metadata. This dynamic substitution reduces code complexity and makes functions highly reusable.

Configuration via function.json

For non-C# functions (e.g., JavaScript, Python), bindings are configured via function.json.

```json
{
  "bindings": [
    {
      "type": "blobTrigger",
      "name": "inputBlob",
      "path": "files/{name}",
      "direction": "in",
      "connection": "AzureWebJobsStorage"
    },
    {
      "type": "queue",
      "name": "outputQueue",
      "queueName": "processed",
      "direction": "out",
      "connection": "AzureWebJobsStorage"
    }
  ]
}
```

Advanced Patterns

Fan-Out/Fan-In (Parallel Processing)

Break large workloads into smaller tasks:

```
[FunctionName("FanOutFunction")]
public static async Task Run(
    [QueueTrigger("batch-jobs")] string batchJob,
    [Queue("individual-tasks")] ICollector<string> taskQueue)
{
```

```
    var tasks =
JsonConvert.DeserializeObject<List<string>>(batchJob);
    foreach (var task in tasks)
    {
        taskQueue.Add(task);
    }
}
```

Another function can then process each `task` from `individual-tasks` queue.

Chaining with Durable Functions

Use Durable Functions to chain function executions and pass data between them without managing state manually.

Testing Triggers and Bindings Locally

- Use Core Tools: `func start`

- Use tools like **Postman**, **curl**, or **Azure Storage Explorer** to test triggers.

- For Queue/Blob/EventGrid, simulate input using the Azure SDK or CLI.

Example for HTTP trigger:

```
curl http://localhost:7071/api/MyHttpFunction?name=Test
```

For blob trigger testing, upload a file into the monitored container via Storage Explorer.

Limitations and Considerations

- Only one trigger per function is allowed.

- Triggers cannot be dynamically added at runtime.

- Binding types and features vary by language.

- Cold starts may delay execution in the Consumption plan.

- Triggers must match binding schema and connection permissions.

Best Practices

- Use meaningful names for parameters and bindings.

- Leverage binding expressions to avoid manual parsing.

- Store connection strings securely in Application Settings or Key Vault.

- Use retry policies and dead-letter queues for Service Bus triggers.

- Keep trigger logic thin—delegate complex logic to services or separate classes.

- Prefer input/output bindings over SDKs when possible for readability and simplicity.

Summary

Triggers and bindings are foundational to building powerful serverless applications in Azure. They enable rapid development by abstracting common integration patterns and reducing boilerplate. Understanding their capabilities, configuration models, and limitations allows developers to construct robust, maintainable solutions that react to a wide array of events and data sources.

From simple HTTP APIs to complex data pipelines and orchestrations, triggers and bindings are the glue that connects your business logic to the broader Azure ecosystem. Mastery of this model sets the stage for building efficient, scalable serverless applications.

Managing Function App Configuration and Deployment

Once your Azure Function is written and tested locally, the next critical step is configuring and deploying it to a production-ready environment. Configuration management ensures your application behaves consistently across environments, while deployment techniques determine how reliably and efficiently your code reaches the cloud.

This section will guide you through managing settings for your Function Apps, using environment-specific configurations, implementing secure secret handling, automating deployments, and monitoring live functions post-deployment. We'll cover deployment strategies, integration with CI/CD pipelines, slot usage, deployment options, and best practices for scalable, maintainable serverless infrastructure.

Understanding the Azure Function App Structure

An Azure Function App is more than just a collection of functions. It's a container that hosts one or more function definitions and provides shared configuration across them.

Key characteristics include:

- All functions in the app share a **runtime version** and **resource plan**.

- The Function App has its own **application settings**, **identity**, and **deployment settings**.

- Configuration changes affect all functions within the same app.

Understanding this scope is essential for organizing your functions effectively, especially in production environments.

Application Settings and Configuration

Application settings in Azure Function Apps act similarly to environment variables. They are essential for storing connection strings, API keys, runtime settings, and feature flags.

You can configure them in several ways:

Using Azure CLI

```
az functionapp config appsettings set \
  --name my-function-app \
  --resource-group my-resource-group \
  --settings "MySetting=value1"
```

Using the Azure Portal

1. Navigate to your Function App.

2. Go to **Configuration** under **Settings**.

3. Add/edit key-value pairs.

Using ARM/Bicep

```
resource functionApp 'Microsoft.Web/sites@2021-02-01' = {
  name: 'myFunctionApp'
  location: resourceGroup().location
  kind: 'functionapp'
  properties: {
```

```
  siteConfig: {
    appSettings: [
      {
        name: 'MySetting'
        value: 'value1'
      }
    ]
  }
}
}
```

Local Configuration: `local.settings.json`

When working locally, settings are stored in `local.settings.json`:

```json
{
  "IsEncrypted": false,
  "Values": {
    "AzureWebJobsStorage": "UseDevelopmentStorage=true",
    "FUNCTIONS_WORKER_RUNTIME": "dotnet",
    "MySetting": "value1"
  }
}
```

Note: This file should **not** be checked into source control if it contains secrets.

To load these values in code:

```
var settingValue = Environment.GetEnvironmentVariable("MySetting");
```

Using Azure Key Vault

To improve security, sensitive data should be stored in Azure Key Vault rather than app settings.

Steps to Integrate:

1. Create a Key Vault and add secrets.

2. Assign a **Managed Identity** to your Function App.

3. Grant the identity `get` permissions on Key Vault secrets.

4. Reference the secret in your app setting using this syntax:

```
@Microsoft.KeyVault(SecretUri=https://myvault.vault.azure.net/secret
s/ApiKey/)
```

Azure will automatically resolve and inject the value at runtime.

Deployment Options

Azure offers a wide range of deployment options tailored for different workflows.

1. Visual Studio and VS Code

For local development and quick deployments:

- Use "Publish to Azure" in Visual Studio.

- Use `func azure functionapp publish` in VS Code.

2. Azure CLI (Manual)

```
func azure functionapp publish my-function-app
```

Packages and pushes code to Azure.

3. GitHub Actions

Ideal for automated CI/CD pipelines. A sample workflow:

```
name: Deploy Azure Function

on:
  push:
    branches:
      - main

jobs:
  build-and-deploy:
    runs-on: ubuntu-latest
    steps:
```

```
- uses: actions/checkout@v2
- uses: Azure/functions-action@v1
  with:
    app-name: 'my-function-app'
    package: '.'
```

This workflow deploys on every push to the `main` branch.

4. Azure DevOps Pipelines

Use build and release pipelines to manage deployment with advanced controls.

5. Zip Deploy

Package and deploy a zipped folder using REST or CLI:

```
func azure functionapp publish my-function-app --publish-local-settings -i --nozip
```

Or zip manually:

```
zip -r functionapp.zip *
az functionapp deployment source config-zip \
  --resource-group my-rg \
  --name my-function-app \
  --src functionapp.zip
```

6. Containers

For complete control over the environment, you can deploy Azure Functions in custom Docker containers.

Dockerfile example:

```
FROM mcr.microsoft.com/azure-functions/dotnet:4
COPY . /home/site/wwwroot
```

Build and push to Azure Container Registry, then configure your Function App to pull from the container image.

Deployment Slots

Azure Functions on Premium or App Service Plans support **deployment slots**. These let you safely test a new version before replacing the production environment.

- Create a **staging slot**.

- Deploy code to the staging slot.

- Verify functionality.

- Swap with the **production** slot.

Benefits:

- Zero-downtime deployment

- Rollback support

- Independent configuration and settings

```
az functionapp deployment slot create \
  --name my-function-app \
  --resource-group my-resource-group \
  --slot staging
```

Swap slots:

```
az functionapp deployment slot swap \
  --name my-function-app \
  --resource-group my-resource-group \
  --slot staging \
  --target-slot production
```

Monitoring and Logs

Monitoring your live Function Apps is essential to ensuring stability and catching issues early.

Application Insights

By default, Azure Functions can integrate with Application Insights:

- View request traces and logs.

- Monitor execution counts and durations.

- Analyze exceptions and failures.

Add logging to your code using `ILogger`:

```
log.LogInformation("Function executed at: {time}", DateTime.UtcNow);
```

Use **KQL (Kusto Query Language)** to explore logs:

```
requests
| where cloud_RoleName == "my-function-app"
| summarize count() by bin(timestamp, 1h)
```

Azure Monitor

Azure Monitor extends insights to include infrastructure metrics:

- Memory and CPU usage

- Scaling operations

- Resource availability

Set up alerts based on metrics to notify teams of abnormal behavior.

Configuration Best Practices

- **Use environment-specific settings** in app configurations.

- **Do not hardcode values**—use environment variables or app settings.

- **Store secrets in Azure Key Vault**.

- **Use deployment slots** for staging and testing.

- **Automate deployments** via GitHub Actions or Azure DevOps.

- **Separate concerns**—one Function App per domain when possible.

- **Use app settings versioning** for rollback capability.

- **Track settings using Infrastructure as Code (IaC)** tools like Bicep or Terraform.

Troubleshooting Deployment Issues

Common deployment challenges include:

- **Mismatched runtime versions**: Verify using `az functionapp show` and match your project runtime.

- **Missing app settings**: Ensure all required keys are configured in Azure.

- **Storage account errors**: Make sure the linked storage account exists and is accessible.

- **CORS issues**: For browser-based apps, configure CORS under Platform Features.

- **Authentication errors**: Verify permissions when using Managed Identity or Key Vault integration.

Use the **Kudu Console** for advanced debugging:

```
https://<your-function-app>.scm.azurewebsites.net
```

Navigate to **Debug Console > CMD** to inspect files, logs, and environment variables.

Summary

Managing configuration and deployment effectively is essential to the success of any Azure Functions-based solution. Whether you're setting environment variables, integrating with Key Vault, deploying through pipelines, or using slots for safe rollouts, these practices shape the reliability and maintainability of your apps.

With an understanding of these tools and strategies, you're now ready to scale beyond local development and operate your serverless applications in robust cloud environments. As you progress through the rest of the book, these techniques will continue to support your real-world scenarios with consistency, security, and agility.

Chapter 3: Logic Apps: Automating Workflows at Scale

What Are Azure Logic Apps?

Azure Logic Apps is a powerful integration platform as a service (iPaaS) designed to automate workflows and business processes through a visual designer and a rich set of prebuilt connectors. It enables developers and non-developers alike to build scalable, reliable workflows that integrate with hundreds of Microsoft and third-party services—without writing or maintaining extensive codebases.

Logic Apps support everything from simple task automation to complex enterprise workflows that span departments, organizations, or systems. With its serverless architecture, Logic Apps automatically scale to meet demand and require no infrastructure management, making it an ideal solution for organizations looking to streamline operations, enforce consistency, and respond to real-time data changes.

Core Concepts of Logic Apps

At its core, a Logic App consists of a **trigger** and one or more **actions**. The workflow begins with a trigger, which initiates the Logic App execution. The subsequent actions represent steps in a business process, executed either sequentially or conditionally, based on the outcome of earlier steps.

1. Trigger

The trigger is the starting point of a Logic App. It defines when the workflow should be initiated. Triggers can be event-based (e.g., receiving an email, detecting a file in a storage container) or time-based (e.g., every hour, every day).

Examples include:

- **HTTP request received**

- **New email in Outlook**

- **Blob uploaded to Azure Storage**

- **Recurrence (CRON schedule)**

2. Actions

Actions are operations performed after the Logic App is triggered. These can be:

- Sending an email

- Writing to a database

- Posting to a webhook

- Executing an Azure Function

- Creating a SharePoint item

- Connecting to third-party services like Salesforce, Twitter, or Slack

Actions can include conditionals, loops, switches, and scopes for error handling or grouping steps logically.

Types of Logic Apps

There are two primary hosting models for Logic Apps:

1. Consumption (Multi-tenant)

- Traditional Logic Apps

- Billed per execution and connector usage

- Auto-scales

- Deployed and run in Azure's multi-tenant infrastructure

- Ideal for standard integration workloads

2. Standard (Single-tenant)

- Runs on App Service Environment or Functions infrastructure

- Uses Azure Functions runtime under the hood

- Offers local development with VS Code

- Fine-grained control over performance, networking, scaling

- Ideal for enterprise-grade workloads needing VNET or private endpoints

When building new solutions, Logic Apps Standard is increasingly recommended due to its flexibility, performance benefits, and developer tooling support.

Advantages of Logic Apps

1. Low-Code Development

With its visual designer, Logic Apps reduce the need for writing boilerplate code. This empowers non-developers or IT pros to automate processes without deep programming knowledge.

2. Rapid Integration

Logic Apps provide **over 600 connectors** for Azure services, Microsoft 365, SAP, SQL, Oracle, Salesforce, Twitter, Dropbox, and more. This vastly reduces time-to-value for integrations.

3. Built-in Resiliency

Retries, timeout handling, and error scopes are built-in, ensuring workflows can gracefully handle transient failures and network issues without custom retry logic.

4. Serverless Scaling

Workflows scale automatically based on demand. There's no need to manage infrastructure, allocate resources, or configure load balancers.

5. First-Class Monitoring and Auditing

Logic Apps integrate natively with Azure Monitor, Log Analytics, and Application Insights, enabling detailed diagnostics, telemetry tracking, and alerting.

6. Compliance and Security

Logic Apps inherit Azure's security posture, including support for:

- Azure Active Directory

- Managed Identities

- Role-Based Access Control (RBAC)

- Virtual Network integration (in Standard plan)

Logic App Designer Overview

The Logic Apps Designer is an intuitive drag-and-drop interface available in both the Azure Portal and Visual Studio Code (for Standard Logic Apps).

Key Features:

- Searchable connector and action library

- Visual branching and conditionals (If, Switch, etc.)

- Scopes for error handling (`Try`, `Catch`, `Finally`)

- Dynamic content mapping between steps

- Expression editor for advanced logic

Workflows are defined in a JSON schema known as **Workflow Definition Language (WDL)**, but the designer abstracts this for most users.

Logic Apps and Connectors

Connectors are wrappers for external services or internal Azure services that define how Logic Apps can interact with them.

Types of Connectors:

- **Standard Connectors**: Free to use, e.g., Azure Blob, HTTP, Delay.

- **Premium Connectors**: Require an integration account or additional licensing, e.g., Salesforce, SAP, Oracle.

- **Enterprise Connectors**: For large-scale systems and protocols like AS2, X12, EDIFACT.

Each connector provides **triggers** and/or **actions**. For example:

- Outlook 365: trigger on new email, action to send email

- Azure Blob Storage: trigger on new blob, action to get blob content

- SQL Server: action to execute stored procedures or queries

Common Logic App Patterns

1. Approval Workflow

- Trigger: SharePoint item created

- Action: Send email to approver

- Condition: Based on response, update item status

- Optional: Send notification to requester

2. File Transfer Pipeline

- Trigger: File uploaded to Blob Storage

- Actions:
  - Get metadata
  - Rename file
  - Move to archive
  - Notify via Teams

3. Social Media Listener

- Trigger: New Tweet with hashtag

- Actions:
  - Analyze sentiment
  - Log to Cosmos DB
  - Notify marketing team

4. API Gateway

- Trigger: HTTP request

- Actions:
  - Call multiple downstream services
  - Aggregate results

    ○   Return composite response

Expressions and Transformations

Logic Apps support inline expressions using **Workflow Definition Language** and **Azure Functions Expressions**. This allows for dynamic data manipulation, conditional logic, and content transformation.

Example expression:

```
"@concat('Hello ', triggerOutputs()?['headers']['x-user-name'])"
```

Expressions are used in:

- Conditions (`if`, `equals`, `contains`)

- String manipulation (`concat`, `substring`)

- Math operations

- Date/time handling

- Iterating over arrays (`foreach`)

Error Handling and Scopes

Logic Apps include built-in mechanisms for handling errors:

- **Scopes**: Group actions and apply conditional logic based on success, failure, or timeout.

- **Run After**: Configure steps to execute only if a prior step succeeds, fails, or is skipped.

- **Retry Policies**: Automatic retries with customizable intervals and limits.

- **Terminate**: Ends the workflow with a success or failure status explicitly.

Example of error scope usage:

```
{
```

```
"type": "Scope",
"actions": {
  "Try": { /* primary logic */ },
  "Catch": {
    "runAfter": {
      "Try": ["Failed"]
    },
    "actions": {
      "SendEmail": { /* alerting logic */ }
    }
  }
}
}
```

Cost Model

Pricing is based on the **number of executions** and **connectors used**.

- **Consumption Logic Apps**: Pay per action and trigger.

- **Standard Logic Apps**: Billed per vCPU-second and memory usage, with fixed baseline costs.

Premium and enterprise connectors add to cost. Carefully consider design to reduce redundant actions, unnecessary polling, or frequent triggers.

Security and Access Control

Security is paramount in enterprise-grade Logic Apps:

- **Authentication**: Support for OAuth2, Basic Auth, API keys, Azure AD

- **Authorization**: Protect HTTP endpoints with function keys or OAuth

- **Managed Identity**: Secure access to Azure services without secrets

- **Private Endpoints**: Limit access to within a VNET

- **Encryption**: All data in transit and at rest is encrypted using Azure standards

Use **API Management** to secure public-facing Logic Apps, applying rate limits, quotas, and JWT validation.

Deployment and DevOps

Logic Apps support deployment via:

- **Azure Portal**: Manual authoring

- **Visual Studio Code**: With Logic Apps Standard extension

- **ARM templates / Bicep / Terraform**: For Infrastructure as Code (IaC)

- **GitHub Actions / Azure DevOps**: CI/CD automation

Use parameterized templates to support environment-specific values (e.g., development, staging, production).

Example GitHub Action deployment:

```
- uses: azure/arm-deploy@v1
  with:
    subscriptionId: ${{ secrets.AZURE_SUBSCRIPTION_ID }}
    resourceGroupName: my-rg
    template: ./logicapp.bicep
```

Summary

Azure Logic Apps provide a low-code, scalable platform for building integration and automation workflows. With hundreds of connectors, powerful built-in actions, error-handling features, and extensive developer tooling, Logic Apps enable rapid delivery of business logic without the complexity of traditional application development.

Whether you're building an approval workflow, orchestrating multi-step API calls, or reacting to real-time data events, Logic Apps serve as the backbone of many modern serverless architectures. The next sections will walk you through designing, integrating, and debugging workflows to harness the full potential of this platform.

Designing Workflows with the Logic Apps Designer

Designing workflows with the Azure Logic Apps Designer is a powerful and accessible way to build scalable, automated processes without writing large amounts of code. The designer provides a visual interface to orchestrate actions, conditions, loops, connectors, and error-handling constructs. This section offers a deep dive into using the Logic Apps Designer, focusing on how to structure workflows effectively, organize steps logically, integrate services, apply conditions and loops, and enforce operational best practices.

Whether you're working in the Azure Portal or developing locally with Visual Studio Code using Logic Apps Standard, mastering the designer is key to building efficient, maintainable, and resilient workflows.

Accessing the Logic Apps Designer

There are two primary environments where you can use the Logic Apps Designer:

1. Azure Portal (Consumption Plan)

- Navigate to your Logic App resource.

- Click on **Logic App Designer**.

- Use the visual editor to create your workflow.

- Save and run workflows directly from the portal.

2. Visual Studio Code (Standard Plan)

- Install the **Azure Logic Apps (Standard)** extension.

- Open or create a Logic App project.

- Use the local designer (embedded in VS Code) to visually build workflows.

- Deploy workflows to Azure using Azure CLI or GitHub Actions.

Workflow Structure: Triggers and Actions

All Logic Apps begin with a **trigger**, followed by one or more **actions**. The structure resembles a flowchart that can branch, loop, or respond to dynamic data inputs.

Trigger

The workflow starts here. The most common triggers include:

- **HTTP request** (for API scenarios)

- **Recurrence** (for scheduled automation)

- **Event-based triggers** (e.g., Blob upload, new email, new tweet)

Example of a Recurrence trigger configuration:

```
"recurrence": {
  "frequency": "Hour",
  "interval": 1
}
```

This sets the Logic App to run every hour.

Actions

Actions are the building blocks of workflow logic. They can:

- Perform HTTP calls

- Send emails

- Write to a database

- Execute Azure Functions

- Manipulate variables

- Parse JSON or XML

- Loop over data

- Branch with conditions

Each action is represented by a tile in the designer and can be dragged, reordered, or configured via GUI.

Designing a Simple Workflow: Email Notification Example

Let's create a workflow that triggers on a new file upload to Azure Blob Storage and sends an email notification.

1. **Trigger**: Blob created in a specific container

2. **Action 1**: Get blob metadata

3. **Action 2**: Send email with metadata info

Steps in the designer:

- Add a Blob trigger (Azure Blob Storage → When a blob is added or modified).

- Configure connection and path (e.g., `uploads/{blobName}`).

- Add the "Send an email" action (Office 365 Outlook).

- Use dynamic content to insert blob name, size, and link into the email body.

Conditional Logic and Branching

Workflows often need to make decisions. The designer allows you to add **Condition** steps, which behave like `if`/`else` statements.

Scenario: Send an approval email only if the uploaded file is a PDF.

1. Add a **Condition** action after the trigger.

Set the condition:

```
blobName ends with '.pdf'
```

2.
3. In the "Yes" branch:

    o Add email or approval action.

4. In the "No" branch:

    o Log or skip the file.

This allows you to build intelligent workflows that respond differently based on data.

Looping Over Data

When dealing with arrays or collections, you can use **For Each** and **Until** loops.

For Each

Used to iterate over a list of items (e.g., all files in a directory, all rows in a dataset).

Steps:

1. Parse a JSON array (e.g., from HTTP response).

2. Use a **For Each** loop to iterate.

3. Inside the loop, access each item via `items('For_each')`.

Example use case:

- Fetch rows from SQL Server.

- Loop through each row and call an external API with the row data.

Until

Executes a block until a condition is met.

- Useful for retry loops, polling external systems, or timeouts.

Example:

- Call an API.

- Wait 10 seconds.

- If status = `completed`, exit.

- Else, repeat.

Scopes and Grouping

Use **Scopes** to logically group steps and control their execution flow.

Types of scopes:

- **Regular Scope**: Groups steps for readability.

- **Try Scope**: Contains steps that may fail.

- **Catch Scope**: Executes if the Try Scope fails.

- **Finally Scope**: Runs regardless of outcome.

Example pattern:

- Scope: Upload files

- If upload fails → run Catch Scope: Send alert

- Always → run Finally Scope: Cleanup temp files

Scopes support the `runAfter` configuration, allowing you to execute based on success, failure, skipped, or timeout conditions of preceding steps.

Using Variables and Data Manipulation

Variables help store, manipulate, and pass data between steps.

Types of variables:

- **String**

- **Boolean**

- **Integer**

- **Array**

- **Object**

To initialize a variable:

```
{
  "type": "InitializeVariable",
  "name": "myVariable",
  "inputs": {
    "name": "counter",
```

```
    "type": "Integer",
    "value": 0
  }
}
```

To update a variable:

```
{
  "type": "IncrementVariable",
  "inputs": {
    "name": "counter",
    "value": 1
  }
}
```

Variables are often used in loops, condition evaluations, and summary reports.

Expressions in the Designer

Use **expressions** to transform data, evaluate logic, and construct strings dynamically.

Common expression functions:

- `concat()` – Combine strings

- `equals()` – Compare values

- `contains()` – Check if a value exists

- `addDays()` – Add or subtract dates

- `json()` – Parse JSON strings

- `length()` – Get array or string length

Example:

```
@concat('Hello ', triggerOutputs()?['headers']['x-user-name'])
```

Expressions are used inside the GUI in fields marked **Add dynamic content → Expression**.

Testing Workflows

Once your workflow is designed:

1. Save the Logic App.

2. Run a manual trigger (for HTTP or Recurrence).

3. View the **Runs history** tab.

4. Click a run to inspect:

   - Inputs

   - Outputs

   - Errors

   - Execution time per step

Each step shows a green (success), red (failure), or gray (skipped) indicator.

Version Control and Deployment

For production environments, develop and store workflows in source control.

In Visual Studio Code:

- Workflows are saved as `.workflow.json` files.

- Check into GitHub or Azure Repos.

- Deploy using:

  - ARM/Bicep templates

  - Azure CLI

  - GitHub Actions

Example CLI deployment:

```
az deployment group create \
```

```
--resource-group my-rg \
--template-file logicapp.bicep \
--parameters environment=dev
```

Best Practices

- **Name actions clearly**: Avoid default names like "Condition 1".

- **Use scopes** for grouping and error control.

- **Avoid unnecessary polling**: Use event-based triggers where possible.

- **Secure endpoints**: Use OAuth, API Management, or Azure AD.

- **Limit nested loops**: Deep nesting can impact readability and performance.

- **Log critical steps**: Use Azure Monitor or Application Insights for telemetry.

- **Use retry policies**: For transient fault tolerance.

- **Avoid hardcoding**: Use parameters, settings, or Key Vault references.

Summary

The Logic Apps Designer empowers users to create powerful workflows visually and intuitively. From simple one-step tasks to multi-branch, multi-connector enterprise processes, the designer abstracts much of the complexity involved in traditional development.

By learning to work with triggers, actions, loops, conditions, scopes, and expressions, you can construct automated workflows that improve productivity, reduce manual tasks, and integrate cloud-native services seamlessly. The next section will explore how to connect Logic Apps to both internal and third-party systems to create robust and extensible automation solutions.

Connecting to Services and APIs

One of the most powerful features of Azure Logic Apps is its ability to integrate seamlessly with a vast array of services—both within and outside of the Microsoft ecosystem. This ability to "connect everything" is what elevates Logic Apps from a simple automation tool to a full-fledged integration platform capable of handling complex, enterprise-grade workflows.

In this section, we'll explore how to connect Logic Apps to services and APIs. We'll cover connectors, authentication methods, custom APIs, third-party integrations, data transformation between systems, and best practices for managing secure and efficient connections.

Understanding Connectors

Connectors in Logic Apps are predefined wrappers for services and APIs that enable you to perform actions or trigger workflows based on external events. Each connector simplifies integration by handling the authentication, request formatting, and error handling for the underlying service.

There are three types of connectors:

- **Standard Connectors** – Core services like HTTP, Azure Blob, OneDrive, SQL Server.

- **Premium Connectors** – Enterprise systems like SAP, Oracle DB, Salesforce.

- **Custom Connectors** – Created by you to integrate with any RESTful API that isn't natively supported.

A connector may support:

- **Triggers** (start the workflow)

- **Actions** (perform tasks within the workflow)

Example:

- Outlook 365: Trigger – new email received; Action – send email.

- SQL Server: Action – execute stored procedure.

Using Built-In Connectors

Logic Apps provides hundreds of out-of-the-box connectors. You can find these by searching in the **Logic App Designer** under the "Choose an operation" panel.

Commonly Used Connectors:

Service	Use Case

Azure Blob Storage	File storage, triggers on blob upload
Office 365 Outlook	Send/receive emails
SharePoint	Add/read/update list items
SQL Server	Execute stored procedures or queries
Dynamics 365	Integrate with CRM systems
Salesforce	Automate sales workflows
Twitter	Social media sentiment analysis
GitHub	Automate DevOps processes

Example: Send an email when a new file is uploaded to Blob Storage.

1. Trigger: Blob created in `uploads/` container

2. Action: Office 365 Outlook → Send Email

3. Email content: uses dynamic fields from the blob (name, URI, size)

Connecting to Azure Services

Logic Apps integrates natively with many Azure resources. These include:

- **Azure Functions** – call serverless functions for custom logic

- **Azure Storage** – handle blobs, tables, and queues

- **Cosmos DB** – store/retrieve documents

- **Event Grid/Event Hub** – handle event-driven architecture

- **Azure SQL Database** – execute stored procedures, run queries

- **Azure Key Vault** – securely manage secrets and credentials

Example: calling an Azure Function

1. Add a "HTTP" action.

2. Use the function's URL.

3. Pass data in JSON format.

4. Use Key Vault to retrieve a function key (if not using anonymous access).

5. Parse the function response with a `Parse JSON` action.

```
{
  "method": "POST",
  "uri": "https://myfunction.azurewebsites.net/api/doWork",
  "headers": {
    "x-functions-key": "@{parameters('functionKey')}"
  },
  "body": {
    "id": "@{triggerBody()?['id']}",
    "timestamp": "@{utcNow()}"
  }
}
```

Authentication Methods

When connecting Logic Apps to services or APIs, you often need to handle authentication. Logic Apps supports several authentication mechanisms:

1. OAuth 2.0

Used with most Microsoft services, Salesforce, GitHub, Google, etc.

*   Authentication is handled interactively when setting up the connection.

*   Tokens are automatically refreshed and stored securely.

2. API Key

Used with services that issue keys for programmatic access.

*   Key is stored in Logic App settings or Key Vault.

- Add key to headers or query string manually.

3. Basic Authentication

Username and password passed in the request header. Not recommended unless over HTTPS and for legacy systems.

4. Managed Identity (Azure AD)

Highly secure and preferred within Azure.

- Assign a system-assigned or user-assigned identity to your Logic App.

- Grant that identity permissions to services like Key Vault, SQL, or Storage.

- Logic App authenticates without storing credentials.

```
"authentication": {
  "type": "ManagedServiceIdentity"
}
```

5. Custom Headers

Add any required headers manually in HTTP actions:

```
"headers": {
  "Authorization": "Bearer @{parameters('accessToken')}"
}
```

Connecting to External APIs

If a third-party service doesn't have a built-in connector, use the **HTTP** action to connect directly to its REST API.

Steps:

1. Get the API endpoint.

2. Review documentation for required headers, method (GET/POST/etc.), and body.

3. Configure the HTTP action with the details.

4. Handle authentication via header or token.

5. Parse the response with `Parse JSON`.

Example: Calling a Weather API

```
{
  "method": "GET",
  "uri":
"https://api.weatherapi.com/v1/current.json?key=@{parameters('weathe
rApiKey')}&q=London"
}
```

You can then use the temperature or condition in the next step of your Logic App.

Custom Connectors

If you need to reuse an external API frequently or across multiple Logic Apps, consider building a **Custom Connector**.

Benefits:

- Centralizes authentication and endpoint configuration.

- Appears in the Logic App Designer like native connectors.

- Improves maintainability and abstraction.

Steps:

1. Define OpenAPI/Swagger spec for your API.

2. Import into Azure as a Custom Connector.

3. Secure with OAuth, API Key, or Managed Identity.

4. Share across Logic Apps via Azure integration.

Data Transformation Between Services

Logic Apps often connect services with mismatched data formats. To bridge these gaps, Logic Apps provide tools like:

1. Compose

Create or transform JSON objects and arrays.

```
{
  "fullName": "@{concat(triggerBody()?['firstName'], ' ',
triggerBody()?['lastName'])}",
  "created": "@{utcNow()}"
}
```

2. Parse JSON

Define a schema to parse API responses and enable structured data access.

Use the "Generate from sample" feature to create the schema automatically.

3. XML Transformation

For XML-based systems, Logic Apps support XML parsing and **XSLT transformations**.

4. Flat File Conversion

For legacy systems, use integration accounts and enterprise connectors to handle flat file (CSV, EDI) parsing.

Example Workflow: Salesforce to SQL Integration

1. **Trigger**: New record created in Salesforce

2. **Action**: Parse record details

3. **Action**: Connect to Azure SQL → Run stored procedure to insert data

4. **Action**: Send notification to Microsoft Teams

5. **Scope**: Catch errors and log to Azure Blob

This connects a SaaS CRM (Salesforce) to a relational database (SQL Server) and integrates a collaboration tool (Teams) for real-time updates.

Error Handling and Retry Policies

When connecting to external systems, failures can happen. Logic Apps offer robust retry and error-handling mechanisms.

Retry Policy

Every action can be configured with:

- Number of retry attempts

- Interval between retries

- Exponential backoff

```
"retryPolicy": {
  "type": "exponential",
  "interval": "PT10S",
  "count": 3
}
```

Error Scopes

- Use **Try-Catch-Finally** patterns with scopes.

- Store failed requests for replay.

- Alert teams via email or messaging when integration fails.

Best Practices

- **Use Managed Identity** where possible for secure, secret-less authentication.

- **Reference API keys from Key Vault**, not inline.

- **Centralize API logic** using Custom Connectors for maintainability.

- **Use Parse JSON** for structured data handling.

- **Avoid hardcoded URIs**—use parameters or config files.

- **Test integrations thoroughly** using mock APIs or Postman.

- **Secure outbound calls** with IP restrictions or API firewalls.

Summary

Logic Apps' strength lies in its ability to integrate and automate across services. With hundreds of connectors and flexible HTTP integration, Logic Apps can communicate with virtually any cloud or on-premises system. Whether you're sending alerts, orchestrating sales workflows, or syncing data across platforms, the connectivity options in Logic Apps give you the power to build seamless, intelligent systems with ease.

In the next section, you'll learn how to debug, monitor, and optimize these workflows, ensuring that your integrations remain stable, performant, and scalable.

Debugging and Monitoring Workflows

Efficient debugging and continuous monitoring are critical components of building reliable workflows with Azure Logic Apps. While creating a workflow is relatively straightforward using the visual designer, ensuring that it runs correctly under all conditions—and identifying what went wrong when it doesn't—is where robust debugging and monitoring tools come into play.

This section provides a comprehensive guide to debugging Logic Apps during development, tracing real-time executions, analyzing failure cases, setting up alerts, using diagnostic tools, and leveraging integrations with Azure Monitor, Log Analytics, and Application Insights for deep observability.

Overview of Monitoring Tools

Azure provides several layers of tooling to help developers and operators monitor Logic App behavior:

- **Logic App Runs History**: Immediate, visual feedback on past executions.

- **Azure Monitor Logs**: Structured logs and metrics for analysis.

- **Application Insights**: Deep telemetry with distributed tracing.

- **Log Analytics**: Search, filter, and aggregate historical logs.

- **Azure Alerts**: Automated notifications for failures or anomalies.

- **Kusto Query Language (KQL)**: Advanced querying and analytics.

Each of these tools serves a distinct purpose, and together they provide a holistic view of your Logic App health and performance.

Reviewing Run History

Each time a Logic App is triggered, it creates an execution instance called a **run**.

To view run history:

1. Navigate to the Logic App in the Azure Portal.

2. Click **Runs history** under **Monitoring**.

3. Select a specific run to view:

    o   Trigger input/output

    o   Action status

    o   Execution time

    o   Errors and diagnostics

Run status indicators:

-   ✓ Succeeded

-   ✗ Failed

-   ☐ Running

-   ⚠☐ Skipped (due to conditionals or errors)

Each step in the workflow shows its own input and output, helping you trace data through the workflow.

Step-by-Step Debugging

To debug effectively:

1. **Use descriptive action names**: This makes it easier to identify issues.

2. **Add Compose actions**: Use Compose steps to inspect data between transformations.

3. **Use Scope blocks**: Group related actions, making debugging logical blocks easier.

4. **Enable error handling**: Add parallel scopes for failure tracking.

5. **Log key values**: Use Azure Monitor or email steps to log diagnostics during the workflow.

Example: Logging input data

Add a `Compose` action at the beginning of the workflow to inspect the trigger input:

```
@triggerBody()
```

You can view this in the run history to verify incoming data before it flows through your logic.

Handling Errors in Workflows

Logic Apps provide multiple ways to handle errors gracefully:

Run After

Each action has a **runAfter** property, which determines if it runs based on the result of previous steps.

```
"runAfter": {
  "PreviousAction": ["Failed"]
}
```

You can configure actions to run:

- Only on success

- Only on failure

- On both

- If the previous step was skipped or timed out

Error Scopes

Use **Try-Catch-Finally** scopes:

- **Try**: Contains main logic

- **Catch**: Activated if any action in Try fails

- **Finally**: Always executes, useful for cleanup

Catch scope example:

```
{
  "type": "Scope",
  "name": "CatchErrors",
  "actions": {
    "SendFailureNotification": {
      "type": "SendEmail",
      "inputs": {
        "To": "admin@example.com",
        "Subject": "Workflow Failed",
        "Body": "Failure in logic app at @{utcNow()}"
      }
    }
  },
  "runAfter": {
    "TryScope": ["Failed"]
  }
}
```

Retries and Timeout Policies

Actions in Logic Apps have built-in retry and timeout settings.

Retry Policy

You can configure how many times an action should retry on failure and the interval between attempts:

```
"retryPolicy": {
  "type": "exponential",
  "interval": "PT10S",
  "count": 3
}
```

Types:

- `none`

- `fixed`

- `exponential` (default)

Timeout

To avoid actions hanging indefinitely, set timeout policies per action:

```
"timeout": "PT1M"
```

If the action doesn't complete in 1 minute, it is terminated and marked as failed.

Enabling Diagnostic Logs

You can enable diagnostics in the **Monitoring > Diagnostic settings** tab for each Logic App.

Options include sending logs and metrics to:

- **Log Analytics workspace**

- **Storage Account**

- **Event Hub**

Enable logs for:

- Workflow runtime logs

- Trigger metrics

- Action execution traces

- Standard/Custom connector usage

Logs are stored under the category `WorkflowRuntime`.

Using Log Analytics

Once diagnostics are enabled, use **Log Analytics** to query execution data across Logic Apps.

Navigate to **Logs** in the Azure Portal and use **KQL (Kusto Query Language)** to analyze data.

Basic query:

```
AzureDiagnostics
| where ResourceType == "WORKFLOWS"
| project TimeGenerated, Resource, Status_s, WorkflowName_s,
OperationName_s
| sort by TimeGenerated desc
```

Failed runs:

```
AzureDiagnostics
| where Status_s == "Failed"
| project TimeGenerated, WorkflowName_s, ErrorCode_s,
CorrelationId_g
```

Application Insights Integration

For deeper observability, especially in **Logic Apps Standard**, integrate with **Application Insights**.

Benefits:

- Distributed tracing

- Custom events and metrics

- Live metrics stream

- Smart failure detection

Setup Steps:

1. Create an Application Insights instance.

2. Link it to your Logic App using the Azure Portal or ARM template.

3. In workflows, use the TrackEvent action to emit custom telemetry:

```
{
  "name": "TrackEvent",
  "inputs": {
    "eventName": "WorkflowStarted",
    "properties": {
      "WorkflowName": "OrderProcessing",
      "StartTime": "@utcNow()"
    }
  }
}
```

View data in **Application Insights > Logs** or create custom dashboards.

Setting Alerts and Notifications

Use **Azure Monitor Alerts** to notify teams of critical issues:

1. Navigate to Azure Monitor.

2. Create a new Alert Rule.

3. Select your Logic App as the resource.

4. Define a condition (e.g., failed runs > 1 in 10 minutes).

5. Assign an action group (email, webhook, SMS, Teams, etc.)

Example:

Trigger: Failure count > 5 in 10 minutes
 Action: Send SMS to on-call engineer

You can also connect alerts to **ServiceNow**, **PagerDuty**, or custom webhooks.

Troubleshooting Scenarios

Trigger Not Firing

- Check trigger history in the Logic App run blade.

- Ensure the event source (e.g., Blob Storage) is active and integrated properly.

- Review trigger conditions and frequency settings.

Authentication Errors

- Re-authenticate connector credentials.

- Use Azure Key Vault to manage secret rotation.

- For Managed Identity, verify RBAC permissions.

Connector Failures

- Review action input/output for malformed payloads.

- Confirm service availability (e.g., Salesforce API not down).

- Use retry policy to mitigate transient faults.

Performance Bottlenecks

- Monitor action duration in run history.

- Avoid nested loops when possible.

- Use **batching** and **parallelism** for high-throughput use cases.

Best Practices for Debugging and Monitoring

- **Use scopes** to isolate failures.

- **Log key variables** using Compose or Application Insights.

- **Enable diagnostic logs** from day one.

- **Set alerts** for failure patterns and performance thresholds.

- **Avoid excessive retries**—some errors are permanent.

- **Use correlation IDs** to trace workflows across systems.

- **Version control** your Logic Apps for rollback and auditability.

- **Capture exceptions** in catch scopes and persist to storage or send to alerting systems.

Summary

Debugging and monitoring are not optional—they are vital for maintaining resilient, production-grade Logic Apps. Azure provides a rich toolkit for tracking execution, diagnosing issues, and maintaining visibility into every aspect of your workflows.

By leveraging Run History, Diagnostic Logs, Application Insights, and proactive alerting, you ensure that workflows are not only functional, but observable, recoverable, and performant. As your automation scales across teams and services, these monitoring practices will become the backbone of operational excellence.

Chapter 4: Developing Real-Time Solutions

Event-Driven Patterns with Event Grid and Azure Functions

In today's cloud-native architectures, responsiveness and agility are critical. Event-driven systems enable real-time communication between decoupled components, allowing systems to react to changes, process data immediately, and scale efficiently. Azure provides powerful tools to implement such architectures, and in this section, we will explore how to build event-driven solutions using **Azure Event Grid** and **Azure Functions**.

Understanding Event-Driven Architecture

At its core, event-driven architecture (EDA) revolves around the production, detection, consumption, and reaction to events. An **event** is a significant change in state—for instance, a file being uploaded, a user signing in, or a payment being processed.

Key characteristics of EDA:

- **Loose coupling**: Producers and consumers of events are unaware of each other.

- **Scalability**: New consumers can be added without impacting producers.

- **Asynchronous processing**: Events are processed without blocking the producer.

- **Real-time response**: Consumers can react immediately to events.

Azure enables this architecture using services like **Event Grid**, **Azure Functions**, **Service Bus**, and **Logic Apps**.

What is Azure Event Grid?

Azure Event Grid is a fully managed event routing service that enables reactive programming in the cloud. It distributes events from sources (publishers) to subscribers (event handlers) and supports both system and custom events.

Core Components:

- **Event Sources**: Services that emit events. Examples include Azure Blob Storage, Azure Resource Manager, and custom applications.

- **Event Subscriptions**: The configuration that tells Event Grid which events to send to which handlers.

- **Event Handlers**: Services that process the events—Azure Functions, Logic Apps, WebHooks, etc.

Key Features:

- Low latency, high throughput

- Native integration with many Azure services

- Support for custom topics

- Built-in retry logic and dead-lettering

Using Azure Functions as Event Handlers

Azure Functions are ideal for handling events due to their serverless, event-driven nature. When combined with Event Grid, they enable highly scalable and reactive systems.

Let's walk through how to build a real-time image processing solution triggered by blob uploads using Event Grid and Azure Functions.

Step-by-Step: Building a Real-Time Image Processor

Scenario

When a new image is uploaded to an Azure Storage container, we want to trigger an Azure Function that analyzes the image and logs metadata.

Step 1: Set Up the Storage Account and Container
Create a storage account:

```
az storage account create --name mystorageaccount --resource-group
myResourceGroup --location westeurope --sku Standard_LRS
```

1.

Create a blob container:

```
az storage container create --name images --account-name
mystorageaccount --public-access off
```

2.

Step 2: Create an Azure Function App

```
az functionapp create --resource-group myResourceGroup --
consumption-plan-location westeurope --runtime node --functions-
version 4 --name ImageProcessorFuncApp --storage-account
mystorageaccount
```

Step 3: Enable Event Grid on the Storage Account

Blob Storage supports Event Grid events natively. Ensure it's enabled:

```
az provider register --namespace Microsoft.EventGrid
az provider register --namespace Microsoft.Storage
```

Step 4: Create the Function with Event Grid Trigger

Inside your Function App project, add a new function:

```
func init ImageProcessorProj --worker-runtime node
cd ImageProcessorProj
func new --name ProcessImage --template "Azure Event Grid trigger"
```

In the generated `ProcessImage/index.js`:

```
module.exports = async function (context, eventGridEvent) {
    const event = eventGridEvent.data;
    context.log(`Blob Created:\n Name: ${event.url}`);
    // You could call an image analysis API or log metadata here
};
```

Step 5: Set Up Event Subscription

```
az eventgrid event-subscription create \
  --name imageUploadSub \
  --source-resource-id /subscriptions/<sub-
id>/resourceGroups/myResourceGroup/providers/Microsoft.Storage/stora
geAccounts/mystorageaccount \
  --endpoint-type azurefunction \
  --endpoint /subscriptions/<sub-
id>/resourceGroups/myResourceGroup/providers/Microsoft.Web/sites/Ima
geProcessorFuncApp/functions/ProcessImage
```

Best Practices for Event Grid and Azure Functions

1. **Use dead-lettering**: Ensure no data is lost in case the handler fails.

2. **Filter events**: Use event filters to avoid unnecessary triggers.

3. **Secure your endpoints**: Use authentication where applicable.

4. **Handle retries gracefully**: Implement idempotency in your functions.

Real-Time Patterns Enabled by Event Grid

Pattern 1: Fan-Out Processing

A single event triggers multiple functions. For example, when a product is added to a catalog:

- One function indexes it in search.

- Another updates recommendation engines.

- A third sends notifications.

This is achieved by subscribing multiple handlers to the same topic.

Pattern 2: Event Chaining

Events trigger a series of dependent actions:

- Event A (user uploads a file) → Function 1 (resizes the image)

- Event B (resized image saved) → Function 2 (analyzes image)

- Event C (analysis complete) → Function 3 (updates DB)

Chaining is often implemented using intermediate storage and topic subscriptions.

Pattern 3: Event Aggregation

Multiple small events are aggregated and processed together, reducing overhead. This may involve queueing or batching logic in Azure Functions.

Advanced: Custom Topics and Domains

In complex applications, system topics are not enough. Custom topics allow you to emit and route your own events.

Create a Custom Topic

```
az eventgrid topic create --name myCustomTopic --resource-group
myResourceGroup --location westeurope
```

Publish a Custom Event

```
az eventgrid event publish --topic-name myCustomTopic --resource-
group myResourceGroup --event-id $(uuidgen) \
  --subject "MyApp/Devices" --event-type "DeviceRegistered" --data
'{"deviceId": "1234"}' --data-version 1.0
```

This flexibility allows you to design sophisticated workflows and decoupled services.

Monitoring and Diagnostics

Event Grid integrates with **Azure Monitor**, **Application Insights**, and **Diagnostic Settings**.

- Enable diagnostics to capture delivery failures and latencies.

- Use **Application Insights** in your Azure Functions to track execution time and exceptions.

- **Event Grid Viewer** is a simple web app template to debug events in real time.

```
az monitor diagnostic-settings create --name "EventGridDiagnostics"
\
  --resource "/subscriptions/<sub-
id>/resourceGroups/myResourceGroup/providers/Microsoft.EventGrid/top
ics/myCustomTopic" \
  --workspace <log-analytics-workspace-id> \
  --logs '[{"category": "AllMetrics", "enabled": true}]'
```

Summary

Event Grid and Azure Functions together enable robust, real-time, event-driven applications that are highly scalable and maintainable. By leveraging native Azure integrations, you can respond instantly to events from virtually any service. Whether you're building a responsive IoT system, a notification engine, or a complex processing pipeline, these tools provide the foundation you need.

As you move forward, consider layering **Logic Apps** or **Durable Functions** for more complex orchestration, and always think through your event handling strategy, especially around **retries**, **dead-lettering**, and **security**.

Streamlining Operations with Logic Apps and Service Bus

Modern cloud solutions often involve the coordination of multiple systems, microservices, and data flows. To manage this complexity, Azure provides robust tools like **Azure Logic Apps** and **Azure Service Bus**, which are particularly powerful when combined. This section explores how these services work together to streamline operations, ensuring reliability, scalability, and maintainability in real-time, event-driven architectures.

The Role of Logic Apps in Integration

Azure Logic Apps is a serverless workflow automation service designed for easy integration across services. It allows developers and non-developers alike to design workflows visually through a drag-and-drop interface or code using ARM/Bicep templates or Logic App Standard.

Logic Apps can:

- Connect to over 600+ connectors (including SaaS and enterprise systems).

- Process and transform data from one format to another.

- React to events from systems like Azure Blob Storage, Event Grid, or Service Bus.

- Invoke APIs, send emails, manage approvals, or orchestrate microservices.

With a low-code approach and enterprise-grade reliability, Logic Apps is an ideal orchestration engine.

Azure Service Bus: Reliable Messaging Backbone

Azure Service Bus is a fully managed enterprise messaging system. It supports message queuing, publish-subscribe topics, dead-lettering, and advanced delivery guarantees.

Key features include:

- **Queues**: Point-to-point communication where a message is processed by a single receiver.

- **Topics and Subscriptions**: Publish-subscribe pattern allowing multiple subscribers to receive messages independently.

- **Sessions and Message Ordering**: Guaranteeing ordered delivery.

- **Dead-Letter Queue (DLQ)**: Automatically routes undeliverable messages for later inspection.

Service Bus is ideal when:

- You need guaranteed delivery and message durability.

- Systems communicate asynchronously.

- You want to decouple application components.

Use Case: Order Processing Pipeline

Let's walk through a real-world example where Logic Apps and Service Bus streamline an e-commerce order pipeline:

Scenario: An e-commerce platform receives orders via a public API. These orders need to be validated, sent to inventory and shipping systems, and finally logged for auditing.

High-Level Architecture

1. Customer places an order via HTTP endpoint.

2. Logic App receives the request and validates it.

3. Validated order is placed on a Service Bus topic.

4. Multiple subscribers (inventory, shipping, auditing) process the order independently.

5. Logic App receives processing confirmations and sends notifications.

Step-by-Step Implementation

Step 1: Create the Service Bus Namespace and Entities

```
az servicebus namespace create --name myOrderNamespace --resource-
group myResourceGroup --location westeurope --sku Standard
```

```
az servicebus topic create --resource-group myResourceGroup --
namespace-name myOrderNamespace --name orderTopic

az servicebus subscription create --resource-group myResourceGroup -
-namespace-name myOrderNamespace --topic-name orderTopic --name
inventorySub

az servicebus subscription create --resource-group myResourceGroup -
-namespace-name myOrderNamespace --topic-name orderTopic --name
shippingSub

az servicebus subscription create --resource-group myResourceGroup -
-namespace-name myOrderNamespace --topic-name orderTopic --name
auditSub
```

Step 2: Create a Logic App for Receiving and Publishing Orders

This Logic App will:

- Receive HTTP POST requests.

- Validate the request.

- Publish a message to the Service Bus topic.

Trigger: HTTP Request
Actions:

1. Parse JSON body for validation.

2. If valid, publish to Service Bus.

Example JSON Schema:

```
{
  "type": "object",
  "properties": {
    "orderId": { "type": "string" },
    "customerId": { "type": "string" },
    "items": {
      "type": "array",
      "items": {
```

```
      "type": "object",
      "properties": {
        "productId": { "type": "string" },
        "quantity": { "type": "integer" }
      },
      "required": ["productId", "quantity"]
    }
  },
  "totalAmount": { "type": "number" }
},
"required": ["orderId", "customerId", "items", "totalAmount"]
}
```

Service Bus Action (inside Logic App):

- Choose **Service Bus – Send message**.

- Select the orderTopic.

- Insert the dynamic content from the parsed request.

This pattern ensures the order is validated and sent to the processing topic reliably.

Step 3: Create Logic Apps to Subscribe to the Topic

Each subscriber (inventory, shipping, audit) gets its own Logic App to handle messages.

Inventory Logic App:

- **Trigger**: Service Bus Topic Subscription (inventorySub)

- **Action**: Call inventory API to reserve items.

Shipping Logic App:

- **Trigger**: Service Bus Topic Subscription (shippingSub)

- **Action**: Call shipping service to schedule delivery.

Audit Logic App:

- **Trigger**: Service Bus Topic Subscription (auditSub)

- **Action**: Log message to database or Azure Table Storage.

This model provides high cohesion in responsibilities and low coupling between components. If the shipping system fails, inventory and audit systems continue unaffected.

Error Handling and Retry Strategies

Both Logic Apps and Service Bus provide built-in resilience features:

- **Dead-lettering**: Messages that fail processing can be moved to a DLQ.

- **Retry Policies**: Logic Apps can retry failed steps automatically.

- **Custom Alerts**: Use Azure Monitor to get alerts when retry thresholds are breached.

You can add additional Logic Apps to process DLQ messages manually or notify an administrator for intervention.

Example: DLQ Processing Logic App

1. Trigger: Timer (every 10 minutes)

2. Action: Peek messages from DLQ

3. Action: Resubmit or log based on content/error

Monitoring and Observability

- Use **Azure Monitor** and **Application Insights** to track Logic App runs and failures.

- **Service Bus Metrics**: Track incoming/outgoing messages, delivery count, active DLQ size.

- **Alerts**: Triggered on high failure rate or DLQ growth.

You can configure diagnostic settings:

```
az monitor diagnostic-settings create --name ServiceBusDiag \
```

```
  --resource /subscriptions/<sub-
id>/resourceGroups/myResourceGroup/providers/Microsoft.ServiceBus/na
mespaces/myOrderNamespace \
  --workspace <log-analytics-id> \
  --logs '[{"category": "OperationalLogs", "enabled": true}]'
```

Advanced Features and Patterns

Session-Based Processing

If your orders need to be processed in sequence (e.g., per customer), use **Service Bus Sessions**. Enable sessions on the topic/subscription and use the customer ID as the session ID.

Correlation IDs

Maintain end-to-end traceability by passing a correlation ID through:

- Logic App workflows
- Service Bus messages
- External APIs

This makes debugging and performance analysis much easier.

Request-Reply Pattern

In some scenarios, you need synchronous-like communication. Combine Logic Apps and Service Bus with response queues or durable storage for correlation.

Security Considerations

- Use **Managed Identity** to authenticate Logic Apps with Service Bus.
- Avoid storing connection strings in clear text.
- Apply **Role-Based Access Control (RBAC)** to restrict access.
- Audit usage and set up alerts for unexpected access patterns.

Example: Grant Logic App access to Service Bus using managed identity

```
az role assignment create \
  --assignee <logic-app-identity-principal-id> \
  --role "Azure Service Bus Data Sender" \
  --scope /subscriptions/<sub-
id>/resourceGroups/myResourceGroup/providers/Microsoft.ServiceBus/na
mespaces/myOrderNamespace
```

Summary

By combining Azure Logic Apps and Service Bus, you can orchestrate complex, reliable, real-time operations with minimal code and high maintainability. This architecture pattern is applicable to many domains: e-commerce, finance, healthcare, logistics, and more.

Benefits include:

- **Scalability**: Each consumer scales independently.

- **Resilience**: Built-in retries and dead-lettering reduce failure risk.

- **Decoupling**: Producers and consumers evolve independently.

- **Observability**: Native integration with Azure Monitor and Log Analytics.

In the next section, we'll expand on how these tools integrate with event-driven architectures at scale and demonstrate practical applications involving alerts, notifications, and webhooks.

Practical Scenarios: Alerts, Notifications, and Webhooks

When building real-time applications, the ability to react to specific events quickly and effectively is critical. Azure provides powerful services that allow developers to integrate alerting mechanisms, send notifications, and trigger downstream workflows using webhooks. This section focuses on the practical implementation of these capabilities within a serverless architecture, using **Azure Monitor Alerts**, **Azure Logic Apps**, **Azure Functions**, and **webhooks**.

We'll explore how these components come together to support various real-world scenarios, from infrastructure monitoring to user engagement and operational automation.

Alerts: Monitoring and Response in Real-Time

Azure Monitor is the foundational monitoring service for all Azure resources. It enables you to collect, analyze, and act upon telemetry data. With it, you can configure **Alerts** based on performance metrics, logs, or resource conditions.

Types of Alerts

- **Metric Alerts**: Triggered when numeric values (e.g., CPU usage, memory, queue length) exceed thresholds.

- **Log Alerts**: Triggered from Azure Log Analytics queries.

- **Activity Log Alerts**: Based on Azure resource-level operations (e.g., VM stop/start, role assignment changes).

Creating a Metric Alert

Let's say you want to trigger a Logic App when a Service Bus queue's length exceeds 500, indicating a backlog.

1. Navigate to **Azure Monitor > Alerts > New alert rule**

2. Set the **Scope** to your Service Bus queue.

3. Choose the signal: `ActiveMessages`.

4. Set the threshold: `Greater than 500`.

5. Action Group: Choose a **Webhook** or **Logic App**.

6. Set the frequency: Evaluate every 5 minutes.

You can use Azure CLI to automate this setup:

```
az monitor metrics alert create \
  --name QueueBacklogAlert \
  --resource "/subscriptions/<sub-
id>/resourceGroups/myResourceGroup/providers/Microsoft.ServiceBus/na
mespaces/myNamespace/queues/myQueue" \
  --condition "avg ActiveMessages > 500" \
  --description "Alert when queue backlog is high" \
  --action "/subscriptions/<sub-
id>/resourceGroups/myResourceGroup/providers/Microsoft.Logic/workflo
ws/ProcessBacklogAlert"
```

Notifications: Email, SMS, and Push Alerts

Once an alert is triggered, the next step is notifying the right audience. This can include administrators, support teams, or customers.

Using Logic Apps to Send Email Notifications

Azure Logic Apps has built-in connectors for:

- Outlook 365

- Gmail

- SendGrid

- SMTP servers

Example Logic App Workflow:

1. **Trigger**: When an HTTP request is received (from Azure Monitor)

2. **Parse**: Extract alert context from JSON payload

3. **Condition**: Check severity level

4. **Send Email**: Using Outlook 365 connector

```
{
  "severity": "Sev2",
  "resource": "myQueue",
  "metric": "ActiveMessages",
  "value": 682
}
```

Email action configuration:

- To: admin@mydomain.com

- Subject: Queue Alert: High Backlog

- Body: "Queue 'myQueue' has exceeded 500 messages. Current count: 682."

This automated workflow ensures timely visibility into issues without manual intervention.

SMS Notifications with Twilio

Logic Apps also integrates with **Twilio**. Set up your Twilio account, and add the connector to your Logic App.

Action configuration:

- Account SID and Auth Token

- To: +441234567890

- Message: "Queue myQueue has a backlog of 682 messages."

This enables critical alerts to reach mobile devices in real time.

Webhooks: Lightweight Event Triggers

Webhooks are HTTP callbacks used to notify external systems when an event occurs. Unlike polling, they push updates instantly.

Azure services like Event Grid, Logic Apps, and Azure Monitor can send webhooks to any public URL. This is useful for triggering:

- CI/CD pipelines

- Chatbots

- External APIs

- IoT devices

- Custom internal systems

Webhook Listener using Azure Function

Let's create a simple webhook receiver in Azure Functions:

```
[FunctionName("WebhookListener")]
public static async Task<IActionResult> Run(
    [HttpTrigger(AuthorizationLevel.Function, "post", Route = null)]
HttpRequest req,
    ILogger log)
{
```

```
    string requestBody = await new
StreamReader(req.Body).ReadToEndAsync();
    dynamic data = JsonConvert.DeserializeObject(requestBody);

    log.LogInformation($"Webhook received: {data}");

    // Perform any custom logic here

    return new OkObjectResult("Received");
}
```

Expose the function using an HTTP trigger and provide its endpoint as the webhook URL.

Using Webhooks in GitHub Actions

Webhooks can trigger CI/CD pipelines. For example, Logic Apps can notify GitHub Actions to rebuild and deploy an app when a resource state changes.

Webhook payload example:

```
{
  "event": "SiteDeployed",
  "site": "frontend-app",
  "timestamp": "2025-04-09T10:15:00Z"
}
```

In `.github/workflows/deploy.yml`, listen for `repository_dispatch`:

```
on:
  repository_dispatch:
    types: [SiteDeployed]

jobs:
  deploy:
    runs-on: ubuntu-latest
    steps:
      - name: Deploy to production
        run: echo "Deploying site: ${{
github.event.client_payload.site }}"
```

This promotes DevOps automation tied to infrastructure events.

Chaining Alerts, Webhooks, and Logic Apps

Let's walk through a practical example combining all three:

Scenario: Notify a DevOps team when the CPU on a VM exceeds 85% for more than 5 minutes, and automatically scale the instance if the condition persists.

Components

- **Metric Alert**: CPU usage threshold

- **Action Group**: Triggers Logic App via webhook

- **Logic App**: Evaluates condition and notifies team

- **Azure Function**: Invokes scale-out operation

Logic App Workflow:

1. Trigger: HTTP Webhook

2. Parse JSON and extract CPU value and resource ID

3. If value > 85%:

    o   Send Microsoft Teams notification via webhook

    o   Call Azure Function to scale out VMSS

Function scaling logic:

```
[FunctionName("ScaleOutVM")]
public static async Task<IActionResult> Run(
    [HttpTrigger(AuthorizationLevel.Function, "post", Route = null)]
HttpRequest req,
    ILogger log)
{
    var computeClient = new ComputeManagementClient(...);
    var scaleSet = await
computeClient.VirtualMachineScaleSets.GetAsync("myResourceGroup",
"myScaleSet");

    scaleSet.Sku.Capacity += 1;
```

```
    await
computeClient.VirtualMachineScaleSets.CreateOrUpdateAsync("myResourc
eGroup", "myScaleSet", scaleSet);

    return new OkObjectResult("Scaled out successfully.");
}
```

Security and Governance for Notifications and Webhooks

Security is crucial when working with webhooks and alerts.

Best practices:

- **Validate incoming webhook signatures** to prevent spoofing.

- **Use HTTPS endpoints**.

- **Leverage Managed Identities** when calling Azure services.

- **Audit actions** using Azure Monitor and Activity Logs.

- **Throttle alerts** to avoid alert storms.

For webhook authentication, include HMAC SHA256 headers or OAuth tokens in requests.

Real-World Examples

Example 1: Server Down Alert

- Azure Monitor detects VM unreachable.

- Logic App sends email, Teams message, and webhook to PagerDuty.

- Azure Function checks logs and attempts to restart the VM.

Example 2: Data Pipeline Delay

- Data Factory pipeline exceeds expected duration.

- Sends webhook to Logic App.

- Logic App escalates to data engineers and opens a ticket in Azure DevOps.

Example 3: Customer Engagement

- A user submits feedback via website form.

- Logic App receives HTTP trigger.

- Sends email to support, logs to Azure Table Storage, and posts to Slack.

Summary

Integrating alerts, notifications, and webhooks into your Azure serverless workflows empowers you to build proactive, real-time, intelligent systems. By combining Azure Monitor, Logic Apps, Functions, and Service Bus, you can respond automatically to any condition, whether it's a performance issue, business event, or user action.

Key Takeaways:

- Alerts help monitor infrastructure and trigger automation.

- Notifications ensure the right people are informed at the right time.

- Webhooks enable seamless external integrations.

- Logic Apps provide the glue between services, supporting both low-code and advanced automation.

As you build out your solutions, think about what events matter most in your systems, and how you can respond to them in a meaningful, secure, and automated way.

Chapter 5: Integration and Orchestration

Combining Logic Apps with Azure Functions

As applications become increasingly distributed and modular, the need for seamless integration and orchestration of services becomes critical. In the serverless world, **Azure Logic Apps** and **Azure Functions** represent two powerful paradigms—low-code workflow automation and event-driven computing. When used together, they offer flexibility, scalability, and precision in managing end-to-end processes across diverse systems.

This section explores how to design solutions that harness the strengths of both platforms. We'll cover architecture patterns, real-world examples, performance considerations, and best practices for combining Logic Apps with Azure Functions to build reliable and maintainable applications.

Understanding the Roles of Logic Apps and Functions

Before combining them, it's important to understand what each service excels at:

- **Logic Apps**:

    - Ideal for orchestrating multi-step workflows.

    - Integrates with over 600 connectors (e.g., Office 365, Salesforce, SAP).

    - Suits business process automation and long-running workflows.

    - Visual workflow designer for ease of use.

- **Azure Functions**:

    - Best for isolated units of computation or transformation.

    - Lightweight, fast-executing, highly scalable.

    - Supports custom code in multiple languages.

    - Great for processing, validation, enrichment, or integrating with custom systems.

When Logic Apps need to perform complex business logic, calculations, or transformations that go beyond the capabilities of connectors and expressions, Azure Functions can step in.

Integration Scenarios

Let's look at some scenarios where Logic Apps and Azure Functions work together:

1. Data Transformation and Enrichment

Logic Apps receives data from a form or an API, but the incoming payload needs to be normalized or enriched with additional information. Instead of doing this in the Logic App, which would be cumbersome using native expressions, it calls an Azure Function to handle the transformation.

2. Custom API Integration

You have a third-party API with a non-standard authentication scheme or requiring special headers and signing. Azure Functions can act as a proxy or middleware that Logic Apps calls.

3. Heavy Computation Offload

If a Logic App needs to perform computationally heavy operations like pricing calculations, tax computation, or AI inference, it can offload that task to an Azure Function.

Hands-On: Building a Combined Workflow

Scenario: Automated Invoice Processing System

- A new invoice PDF is uploaded to Azure Blob Storage.

- Logic App is triggered by the Blob creation.

- The Logic App sends the PDF file to an Azure Function.

- The Function extracts metadata from the PDF using OCR.

- Logic App stores the metadata in Azure SQL Database and sends a summary email to finance.

Step-by-Step Implementation

Step 1: Create the Azure Function

Let's assume we're using JavaScript to extract text from PDF.

```
const { Readable } = require('stream');
```

```javascript
const pdfParse = require('pdf-parse');

module.exports = async function (context, req) {
    const buffer = Buffer.from(req.body.fileContent, 'base64');
    const data = await pdfParse(buffer);

    const lines = data.text.split('\n').filter(line =>
line.trim().length > 0);
    const invoiceData = {
        invoiceNumber: lines.find(line => line.includes('Invoice
#')).split(':')[1].trim(),
        totalAmount: lines.find(line =>
line.includes('Total')).split(':')[1].trim(),
        date: lines.find(line =>
line.includes('Date')).split(':')[1].trim()
    };

    context.res = {
        status: 200,
        body: invoiceData
    };
};
```

Deploy this Function and get its endpoint URL.

Step 2: Create the Logic App Workflow

1. **Trigger**: When a blob is added to container (e.g., invoices).

2. **Action**: Get file content.

3. **Action**: Call Azure Function

    ○ Method: POST

    ○ Body: { "fileContent":
       "@{base64(body('Get_blob_content'))}" }

4. **Action**: Parse response and extract invoiceNumber, totalAmount, date.

5. **Action**: Insert into SQL using Azure SQL connector.

6. **Action**: Send email using Outlook/Gmail connector.

This approach keeps Logic App's workflow clean and delegates compute-heavy or specialized logic to the Function.

Reusability and Modularity

Using Azure Functions as modular units helps in reusability across Logic Apps:

- A **currency converter** function can be reused in multiple workflows.

- A **custom authenticator** function can standardize API access.

- A **document parser** can serve several business domains (invoices, receipts, contracts).

You can deploy these Functions as part of a shared library and version-control them independently from Logic Apps.

Performance Considerations

When combining Logic Apps with Functions, consider:

- **Cold start latency** in Azure Functions (especially in Consumption plan).

- **Timeout limits**: Logic Apps wait 120 seconds max for synchronous HTTP response.

- **Payload size**: HTTP request/response body limits are around 100 MB.

- **Authentication**: Use Managed Identity for secure, credential-less communication.

To reduce cold starts, consider:

- Using **Premium plan** for Azure Functions.

- Adding a **Timer Trigger** that pings the Function periodically to keep it warm.

Error Handling and Retry Strategy

It's critical to design for failure:

Logic App to Function Integration

- Add a **scope** around the Azure Function call.

- Implement `Run After` conditions to catch failures.

- Retry policy (default): 4 retries, exponential backoff.

Sample configuration:

```
{
  "retryPolicy": {
    "type": "exponential",
    "interval": "PT10S",
    "count": 3
  }
}
```

Function Error Management

In the Function code, always return meaningful HTTP status codes:

- `200 OK` for success

- `400 Bad Request` for client errors

- `500 Internal Server Error` for processing failures

This enables Logic Apps to handle each outcome appropriately.

Monitoring and Observability

Combining Logic Apps and Functions means you need observability across both layers.

- Enable **Application Insights** for Azure Functions.

- Use **Run History** and **diagnostic logs** in Logic Apps.

- Correlate workflows using **custom tracking IDs** passed in headers or request body.

Example: Pass a `correlationId` from Logic App to Function and log it on both sides for traceability.

```
context.log(`Processing request with correlation ID:
${req.headers['x-correlation-id']}`);
```

Security Best Practices

- Use **Azure Active Directory** and **Managed Identities** instead of static keys.

- **Restrict access** to Azure Functions by IP or using Private Endpoints.

- Store secrets (e.g., API keys, connection strings) in **Azure Key Vault** and reference them in Logic Apps and Functions securely.

To allow a Logic App to call a Function securely:

1. Assign a Managed Identity to the Logic App.

2. Grant that identity the `Function App Contributor` role on the Function.

3. Configure the Function to use **Azure AD authentication**.

Advanced Use Case: Order Fulfillment Workflow

1. **Trigger**: New order placed in an e-commerce app.

2. **Logic App**:

   ○ Validates order.

   ○ Calls Azure Function to calculate shipping cost based on weight and distance.

   ○ Calls another Function to apply discount logic.

   ○ Updates inventory using SQL or API.

   ○ Sends order confirmation email.

   ○ Triggers a Service Bus message to notify warehouse.

In this example:

- Logic App manages orchestration, monitoring, and integration.

- Functions encapsulate business logic and allow code-level control.

This separation of concerns improves maintainability and allows teams to work in parallel (workflow vs. compute logic).

Summary

Combining Azure Logic Apps and Azure Functions provides a powerful foundation for serverless integration and orchestration. Logic Apps shine in workflow composition, connector-based integration, and business process automation, while Azure Functions offer flexibility, speed, and the ability to inject custom logic wherever needed.

Benefits of this approach:

- Clean separation of orchestration and logic.

- Improved maintainability and testing.

- Reuse of Functions across workflows.

- Scalable, event-driven, and reactive architecture.

As you design complex cloud-native systems, embrace this combination to handle diverse scenarios—from API integrations to intelligent automation—while keeping your solution modular, secure, and future-proof.

Durable Functions for Long-Running Processes

When dealing with long-running operations in the cloud, traditional stateless functions such as Azure Functions face challenges. These challenges include maintaining state across function executions, handling retries gracefully, coordinating steps across different services, and ensuring reliability even if the workflow spans hours or days. **Durable Functions**, an extension of Azure Functions, solve these challenges by enabling stateful orchestrations in a serverless environment.

This section explores Durable Functions in detail, covering patterns, use cases, implementation strategies, and best practices for building scalable and resilient long-running workflows on Azure.

What Are Durable Functions?

Durable Functions are an extension of Azure Functions that enable you to write stateful workflows using code. This means you can define complex, multi-step processes in code that maintain their state even after the function instance has exited.

Durable Functions are built on top of the **Durable Task Framework**, a reliable framework that handles state persistence, checkpointing, and restarts automatically.

Key Concepts:

- **Orchestrator Function**: The brain of the workflow that defines the sequence of actions.

- **Activity Functions**: The individual tasks or steps in the process.

- **Client Function**: The entry point used to start an orchestration.

- **Entity Functions**: Represent stateful objects with custom operations (optional but powerful).

- **Durable Timer**: Enables delays and timeouts in orchestrations.

Durable Functions are ideal for:

- Approval workflows

- Batch data processing

- Human-in-the-loop processes

- Time-based delays and reminders

- External system coordination

Durable Function Patterns

1. Function Chaining

A sequence of functions are executed in a specific order. Each function depends on the output of the previous one.

```
public static async Task<string> Run(
    [OrchestrationTrigger] IDurableOrchestrationContext context)
{
```

```csharp
    string input = context.GetInput<string>();
    string step1Result = await
context.CallActivityAsync<string>("StepOne", input);
    string step2Result = await
context.CallActivityAsync<string>("StepTwo", step1Result);
    return step2Result;
}
```

2. Fan-Out/Fan-In

Run multiple functions in parallel and then aggregate their results.

```csharp
public static async Task<int> Run(
    [OrchestrationTrigger] IDurableOrchestrationContext context)
{
    var tasks = new List<Task<int>>();
    var inputs = context.GetInput<List<int>>();
    foreach (int input in inputs)
    {
        tasks.Add(context.CallActivityAsync<int>("ProcessItem",
input));
    }
    await Task.WhenAll(tasks);
    return tasks.Sum(t => t.Result);
}
```

3. Async HTTP APIs

Start a process via HTTP and allow the client to poll for status or receive a callback when complete.

```csharp
[FunctionName("StartOrchestration")]
public static async Task<HttpResponseMessage> Start(
    [HttpTrigger(AuthorizationLevel.Function, "post")]
HttpRequestMessage req,
    [DurableClient] IDurableOrchestrationClient starter)
{
    string instanceId = await
starter.StartNewAsync("OrchestrationName", null);
    return starter.CreateCheckStatusResponse(req, instanceId);
}
```

Implementing a Real-World Use Case

Use Case: Employee Onboarding Workflow

Steps involved:

1. Create employee record.

2. Send welcome email.

3. Create Azure AD account.

4. Assign licenses.

5. Notify HR and IT departments.

Some steps are fast (email), others involve external systems (AD), and some require human interaction (approvals).

Step 1: Define Activity Functions

Each step in the process is implemented as a separate activity function.

SendWelcomeEmail.cs

```
[FunctionName("SendWelcomeEmail")]
public static void Run([ActivityTrigger] string employeeEmail,
ILogger log)
{
    log.LogInformation($"Sending welcome email to {employeeEmail}");
    // Email logic here
}
```

CreateAzureADAccount.cs

```
[FunctionName("CreateAzureADAccount")]
public static async Task<string> Run([ActivityTrigger] string
employeeId, ILogger log)
{
    // Call external API to provision account
    return "aad_user_1234";
```

```
}
```

Step 2: Define the Orchestrator

OnboardingOrchestrator.cs

```
[FunctionName("OnboardingOrchestrator")]
public static async Task Run(
    [OrchestrationTrigger] IDurableOrchestrationContext context)
{
    var employee = context.GetInput<Employee>();

    await context.CallActivityAsync("SendWelcomeEmail",
employee.Email);
    var aadUser = await
context.CallActivityAsync<string>("CreateAzureADAccount",
employee.Id);
    await context.CallActivityAsync("AssignLicenses", aadUser);
    await context.CallActivityAsync("NotifyHR", employee.Id);
    await context.CallActivityAsync("NotifyIT", employee.Id);
}
```

Step 3: Start the Workflow

HttpStart.cs

```
[FunctionName("StartOnboarding")]
public static async Task<HttpResponseMessage> Run(
    [HttpTrigger(AuthorizationLevel.Function, "post")] HttpRequest
req,
    [DurableClient] IDurableOrchestrationClient client)
{
    string requestBody = await new
StreamReader(req.Body).ReadToEndAsync();
    var employee =
JsonConvert.DeserializeObject<Employee>(requestBody);

    string instanceId = await
client.StartNewAsync("OnboardingOrchestrator", employee);
```

```
    return client.CreateCheckStatusResponse(req, instanceId);
}
```

Now you have a complete, stateful onboarding workflow that spans multiple services and steps, all orchestrated reliably.

Handling Timeouts and Delays

Durable Functions can wait for specified durations using **Durable Timers**. This is perfect for timeouts or reminders.

```
DateTime deadline = context.CurrentUtcDateTime.AddHours(1);
await context.CreateTimer(deadline, CancellationToken.None);
```

You can also implement **approval timeouts**:

```
var approvalTask = context.WaitForExternalEvent("ManagerApproved");
var timeoutTask = context.CreateTimer(deadline,
CancellationToken.None);

var winner = await Task.WhenAny(approvalTask, timeoutTask);

if (winner == timeoutTask)
{
    await context.CallActivityAsync("SendTimeoutNotification",
employeeId);
}
```

Error Handling and Retries

Durable Functions support built-in retry policies for activity functions:

```
var retryOptions = new RetryOptions(TimeSpan.FromSeconds(5), 3)
{
    Handle = ex => ex is TransientException
};

await context.CallActivityWithRetryAsync("CreateAzureADAccount",
retryOptions, employeeId);
```

You can also catch and react to exceptions in orchestrators:

```
try
{
    await context.CallActivityAsync("RiskyOperation", null);
}
catch (Exception ex)
{
    await context.CallActivityAsync("HandleError", ex.Message);
}
```

Monitoring and Diagnostics

Monitor Durable Functions using:

- **Application Insights**: Logs, traces, performance.

- **Durable Functions Monitor**: A web-based dashboard.

- **Azure Portal**: View orchestration status, replays, and failures.

Enable diagnostic logs:

```
az monitor diagnostic-settings create \
  --name DurableLogs \
  --resource /subscriptions/<sub-
id>/resourceGroups/myResourceGroup/providers/Microsoft.Web/sites/myF
unctionApp \
  --workspace <log-analytics-id> \
  --logs '[{"category": "FunctionAppLogs", "enabled": true}]'
```

Best Practices

- **Keep orchestrators deterministic**: No I/O, logging, random values, or current time.

- **Break down large workflows**: Modularize complex flows into sub-orchestrations.

- **Use external event triggers** for human-in-the-loop processes.

- **Avoid long-running synchronous HTTP calls** inside orchestrators.

- **Secure endpoints** with authentication and validate inputs.

Summary

Durable Functions unlock powerful capabilities for building resilient, long-running workflows in the cloud. Whether you're coordinating multiple APIs, integrating with external systems, or managing human approvals, Durable Functions provide a stateful, scalable solution within the serverless ecosystem.

Benefits include:

- Native orchestration with Azure Functions.

- Scalable and fault-tolerant execution.

- Built-in support for retries, timeouts, and parallelism.

- Reduced infrastructure overhead.

By mastering Durable Functions, developers can confidently build enterprise-grade workflows that run for seconds, minutes, or even days without worrying about state persistence, reliability, or orchestration complexity.

Chaining and Error Handling in Complex Flows

In large-scale distributed systems, workflows often span multiple services and require precise coordination, error recovery, and branching logic. In serverless environments like Azure, chaining various services—such as Functions, Logic Apps, Service Bus, Event Grid, and more—requires careful orchestration to ensure that workflows are both **resilient** and **maintainable**.

This section focuses on how to effectively **chain serverless components** together and implement robust **error handling** mechanisms to build reliable complex flows. We will explore real-world scenarios, architectural patterns, and Azure-native tools that help achieve this with minimal overhead and maximum flexibility.

Chaining in Serverless Architectures

Chaining refers to the act of linking multiple execution steps in a sequence where the output of one component serves as the input for the next. In Azure, chaining can occur across:

- Azure Functions

- Logic Apps

- Durable Functions

- Event Grid events

- Service Bus messages

- Storage Queues

- REST APIs

Properly implemented chaining enables modular workflows and makes systems easier to scale and troubleshoot.

Chaining with Logic Apps

Logic Apps natively support sequential workflows. Here's a simple example:

Scenario: An HR system automatically processes new job applications:

1. Trigger: New file uploaded to Blob Storage.

2. Step 1: Call Azure Function to parse the resume.

3. Step 2: Insert applicant data into SQL Database.

4. Step 3: Send email to HR.

5. Step 4: Post summary to Microsoft Teams.

Each step depends on the previous one. If one fails, the rest must not continue.

```
{
  "definition": {
    "$schema": "...",
    "actions": {
      "ParseResume": {
        "type": "Function",
        "inputs": {
          "method": "POST",
```

```
            "uri": "https://myfunction.azurewebsites.net/api/parse-
resume",
            "body": "@{triggerBody()}"
        },
        "runAfter": {}
    },
    "InsertIntoDatabase": {
        "type": "Sql",
        "inputs": {
            "parameters": {
                "query": "INSERT INTO Applicants ..."
            }
        },
        "runAfter": {
            "ParseResume": ["Succeeded"]
        }
    },
    "SendEmail": {
        "type": "Outlook",
        "inputs": {
            "to": "hr@company.com",
            "subject": "New Applicant"
        },
        "runAfter": {
            "InsertIntoDatabase": ["Succeeded"]
        }
    }
  }
 }
}
```

This example shows how each action is conditionally triggered based on the success of the previous one.

Chaining with Azure Functions

In code-first workflows, you can chain Azure Functions by calling them from each other via HTTP or durable orchestrations.

Simple HTTP chaining example:

```
[FunctionName("StepOne")]
public static async Task<IActionResult> StepOne(
    [HttpTrigger(AuthorizationLevel.Function, "post")] HttpRequest
req)
{
    var data = await new StreamReader(req.Body).ReadToEndAsync();
    var stepTwoResponse = await
httpClient.PostAsync("https://.../StepTwo", new
StringContent(data));
    var result = await stepTwoResponse.Content.ReadAsStringAsync();
    return new OkObjectResult(result);
}
```

However, this approach lacks built-in retry and state tracking. For advanced workflows, prefer **Durable Functions** or Logic Apps.

Chaining with Durable Functions

Durable Functions provide the most powerful mechanism for chaining with built-in fault tolerance and checkpointing.

Example of sequential chaining:

```
[FunctionName("MainOrchestrator")]
public static async Task Run(
    [OrchestrationTrigger] IDurableOrchestrationContext context)
{
    var data = context.GetInput<string>();
    var step1 = await context.CallActivityAsync<string>("StepOne",
data);
    var step2 = await context.CallActivityAsync<string>("StepTwo",
step1);
    var step3 = await context.CallActivityAsync<string>("StepThree",
step2);
}
```

Each activity is retried automatically on transient failures. If the orchestration restarts, it resumes from the last successful checkpoint.

Event-Driven Chaining with Event Grid

Another method of chaining is via **event-driven architecture**:

1. Blob is uploaded → Event Grid fires

2. Function A runs and writes to Storage Queue

3. Queue triggers Function B

4. Function B pushes to Event Grid again

5. Logic App consumes the second event

Each function or service acts independently, responding to events, ensuring loose coupling and scalability.

Error Handling Strategies

In complex flows, things **will** go wrong: APIs may fail, services may be unavailable, data may be malformed. Azure provides several ways to catch and handle errors gracefully.

Logic Apps Error Handling

Logic Apps support `runAfter`, `scope`, and `terminate` actions for error handling.

Example:

```
"ParseResume": {
  "runAfter": {},
  "type": "Function",
  "inputs": {...}
},
"HandleFailure": {
  "runAfter": {
    "ParseResume": ["Failed"]
  },
  "type": "SendEmail",
  "inputs": {
    "to": "support@company.com",
    "subject": "Resume Parsing Failed"
  }
}
```

You can also use **Scopes** to group actions:

- Success/failure states apply to the entire scope.

- Great for try/catch-like logic.

Example structure:

```
"TryScope": {
  "actions": {
    "Step1": {...},
    "Step2": {...}
  }
},
"CatchScope": {
  "runAfter": {
    "TryScope": ["Failed"]
  },
  "actions": {
    "LogError": {...},
    "NotifyOps": {...}
  }
}
}
```

Azure Functions Error Handling

Azure Functions should handle errors by:

- Catching exceptions

- Logging errors

- Returning proper HTTP codes

- Retrying or failing gracefully

Example with retry logic in Durable Functions:

```
var retryOptions = new RetryOptions(TimeSpan.FromSeconds(10), 5)
{
    Handle = ex => ex is HttpRequestException
```

```
};

await context.CallActivityWithRetryAsync("DownloadDocument",
retryOptions, documentUrl);
```

This ensures that transient errors don't break the whole workflow.

Retry and Dead Lettering with Service Bus

If chaining includes Service Bus, use **dead-letter queues (DLQs)** to handle message failures.

Service Bus settings:

- Max delivery count: 10

- Retry policy: exponential

- Enable DLQ

Process DLQs using Logic Apps:

- Trigger: Recurrence (e.g., every 5 minutes)

- Action: Peek or receive from DLQ

- Action: Log to Storage or notify support

This lets you maintain flow without losing messages during downstream outages.

Best Practices

1. **Design for Idempotency**
   Each step in a chain should be repeatable without adverse effects. This ensures retries don't produce inconsistent results.

2. **Implement Compensation Logic**
   For workflows involving side effects (e.g., financial transactions), define rollback or compensating actions.

3. **Use Monitoring and Tracing**
   Add correlation IDs across services. Use App Insights, Log Analytics, or a custom

dashboard for observability.

4. **Segment Workflows by Responsibility**
   Don't build massive monolithic flows. Break them into modular chains with clearly defined inputs/outputs.

5. **Incorporate Alerting**
   Logic Apps and Functions can send alerts on failure. Use Azure Monitor and Alerts to notify engineers of anomalies.

6. **Graceful Degradation**
   Allow partial success in some cases. For example, if non-critical actions fail (e.g., email notification), allow the main workflow to complete.

Real-World Example: Document Processing Chain

Goal: Ingest scanned documents, extract data, validate, and store results.

Steps:

1. Blob upload triggers Event Grid

2. Logic App gets metadata

3. Azure Function extracts text

4. Function calls a third-party validation API

5. Logic App stores validated data in Cosmos DB

6. Sends notification to operations team

Error Handling Plan:

- Step 3 failures → retry 3x, then notify team

- Step 4 failure (validation API) → skip and mark for manual review

- Cosmos DB write failure → route document to retry queue

This kind of chaining with built-in contingencies ensures that the process is robust and production-ready.

Summary

Chaining and error handling are core components of building resilient, scalable serverless applications. Whether using Logic Apps, Azure Functions, or event-driven messaging systems, the ability to reliably link multiple components and gracefully recover from failure is critical.

Key Takeaways:

- Logic Apps are ideal for visual, declarative chaining with built-in error handling.

- Durable Functions provide powerful stateful workflows with advanced retry and error handling.

- Event Grid and Service Bus allow decoupled chaining of independent systems.

- Always plan for errors—fail fast, log early, and recover smoothly.

- Monitor, trace, and alert on your workflows to ensure operational transparency.

By mastering these techniques, you can design complex workflows that are modular, self-healing, and maintainable in the face of unpredictable cloud environments.

Chapter 6: DevOps and CI/CD for Serverless Apps

Infrastructure as Code: Bicep and ARM Templates

As serverless applications scale and evolve, managing infrastructure manually becomes inefficient, error-prone, and difficult to maintain. Infrastructure as Code (IaC) is a foundational DevOps practice that solves this problem by allowing teams to define and manage infrastructure through declarative templates. On Azure, the two primary IaC tools are Azure Resource Manager (ARM) templates and Bicep, a domain-specific language (DSL) that simplifies ARM template authoring.

This section provides a deep dive into using Bicep and ARM templates to provision, manage, and version control your Azure infrastructure for serverless applications. We'll explore core concepts, syntax, best practices, and hands-on examples for deploying Function Apps, Logic Apps, and supporting resources.

Why Infrastructure as Code?

IaC allows infrastructure to be:

- **Version Controlled**: Infrastructure definitions are stored in source control, enabling rollback and collaboration.

- **Repeatable and Consistent**: Environments can be recreated across stages (dev, test, prod) with consistency.

- **Auditable**: All changes are visible and traceable.

- **Automated**: Supports CI/CD pipelines for faster, safer deployments.

With serverless, where services are often created dynamically and scaled rapidly, IaC becomes even more critical for governance and maintainability.

Introduction to ARM Templates

ARM (Azure Resource Manager) templates are JSON-based declarative files that define the resources you want to deploy. They are robust and widely supported across Azure services but can be verbose and harder to manage for complex deployments.

Example: Basic Function App ARM Template

```json
{
  "$schema": "https://schema.management.azure.com/schemas/2019-04-
01/deploymentTemplate.json#",
  "contentVersion": "1.0.0.0",
  "parameters": {
    "functionAppName": {
      "type": "string"
    },
    "location": {
      "type": "string",
      "defaultValue": "West Europe"
    }
  },
  "resources": [
    {
      "type": "Microsoft.Web/sites",
      "apiVersion": "2021-02-01",
      "name": "[parameters('functionAppName')]",
      "location": "[parameters('location')]",
      "kind": "functionapp",
      "properties": {
        "siteConfig": {
          "appSettings": [
            {
              "name": "FUNCTIONS_EXTENSION_VERSION",
              "value": "~4"
            }
          ]
        },
        "serverFarmId": "[resourceId('Microsoft.Web/serverfarms',
'myAppServicePlan')]"
      }
    }
  ]
}
```

While powerful, this syntax can be hard to read and maintain for large deployments, especially when using nested templates or complex conditions.

Introducing Bicep

Bicep is a higher-level abstraction over ARM templates. It simplifies the syntax, improves readability, and provides better tooling and modularity. Bicep transpiles to ARM, maintaining compatibility with Azure's deployment engine.

Bicep is designed to be:

- **Declarative**: You describe what to deploy, not how.

- **Concise**: Fewer lines of code compared to ARM templates.

- **Modular**: Supports reusable modules.

- **Integrated**: Supported directly by Azure CLI, Azure PowerShell, and Azure DevOps.

Installing Bicep

You can install Bicep using the Azure CLI:

```
az bicep install
```

Verify installation:

```
az bicep version
```

Or use `bicep` standalone on macOS/Linux via Homebrew:

```
brew tap azure/bicep
brew install bicep
```

Example: Function App with Bicep

```
param functionAppName string
param location string = 'West Europe'

resource storageAccount 'Microsoft.Storage/storageAccounts@2022-09-
01' = {
  name: '${functionAppName}sa'
  location: location
  sku: {
    name: 'Standard_LRS'
```

```
  }
  kind: 'StorageV2'
}

resource hostingPlan 'Microsoft.Web/serverfarms@2022-03-01' = {
  name: '${functionAppName}-plan'
  location: location
  sku: {
    name: 'Y1'
    tier: 'Dynamic'
  }
}

resource functionApp 'Microsoft.Web/sites@2022-03-01' = {
  name: functionAppName
  location: location
  kind: 'functionapp'
  properties: {
    serverFarmId: hostingPlan.id
    siteConfig: {
      appSettings: [
        {
          name: 'AzureWebJobsStorage'
          value: storageAccount.properties.primaryEndpoints.blob
        }
        {
          name: 'FUNCTIONS_EXTENSION_VERSION'
          value: '~4'
        }
      ]
    }
  }
}
```

To deploy this Bicep template:

```
az deployment group create --resource-group myResourceGroup --
template-file main.bicep --parameters functionAppName=my-func-app
```

Bicep Modules and Reusability

Bicep supports modules, which are reusable components. For example, you can create a `functionApp.bicep` module and reference it in multiple templates.

`main.bicep`:

```
module functionAppModule './functionApp.bicep' = {
  name: 'deployFunctionApp'
  params: {
    functionAppName: 'myApp'
    location: 'West Europe'
  }
}
```

This modular approach promotes reuse and makes large projects more manageable.

Best Practices

- **Use Parameters and Variables**: Avoid hardcoding values to enable flexibility.

- **Structure with Modules**: Break down large deployments.

- **Validate and Lint**: Use `bicep build` and `bicep lint` to catch errors early.

- **Source Control Everything**: Treat IaC files like source code.

- **Automate Deployment**: Integrate templates into CI/CD pipelines.

CI/CD Pipeline Integration

Both ARM and Bicep templates can be deployed in automated pipelines using GitHub Actions or Azure DevOps.

Example GitHub Action Workflow:

```
name: Deploy Function App

on:
  push:
    branches:
      - main
```

```
jobs:
  deploy:
    runs-on: ubuntu-latest
    steps:
      - name: Checkout code
        uses: actions/checkout@v2

      - name: Azure Login
        uses: azure/login@v1
        with:
          creds: ${{ secrets.AZURE_CREDENTIALS }}

      - name: Deploy Bicep Template
        run: |
          az deployment group create \
            --resource-group myResourceGroup \
            --template-file ./infrastructure/main.bicep \
            --parameters functionAppName=my-func-app
```

Choosing Between ARM and Bicep

Feature	ARM Templates	Bicep
Format	JSON	Custom DSL
Readability	Low	High
Tooling	Good	Excellent
Learning Curve	Steep	Gentle
Modularity	Basic	Strong
Official Support	Full	Full

Unless your team already has a strong investment in ARM templates, Bicep is generally the preferred choice for new projects due to its ease of use and modern capabilities.

Final Thoughts

Infrastructure as Code is a non-negotiable best practice for modern serverless development. Whether you choose ARM templates or Bicep, the benefits in terms of automation, repeatability, and maintainability are clear. With Bicep rapidly maturing and fully supported by Azure, it's the ideal tool to provision your Function Apps, Logic Apps, Storage Accounts, Key Vaults, and more.

Mastering IaC with Bicep not only improves your developer workflow but also lays the foundation for robust CI/CD pipelines, secure deployments, and scalable systems. As you progress, consider integrating policy-as-code (e.g., Azure Policy), secrets management (Key Vault), and test automation to further enhance your DevOps practice.

Setting Up GitHub Actions and Azure DevOps Pipelines

The deployment and lifecycle management of serverless applications demand automation, repeatability, and transparency. Continuous Integration and Continuous Deployment (CI/CD) pipelines allow you to build, test, and deploy serverless solutions with minimal manual intervention, ensuring high-quality releases and fast iterations.

In this section, we'll explore how to set up CI/CD pipelines using **GitHub Actions** and **Azure DevOps Pipelines** to automate deployments of Azure Functions, Logic Apps, and supporting infrastructure. We'll look at the necessary configurations, secrets management, testing strategies, and deployment patterns tailored to serverless applications.

The Role of CI/CD in Serverless

Serverless development is often fast-paced, with frequent iterations across multiple environments. Without automation, you may face:

- Deployment inconsistencies between environments.

- Manual errors and oversights.

- Lack of traceability for releases.

- Difficulty in enforcing compliance and testing policies.

With CI/CD, you gain:

- **Automated provisioning** of infrastructure and services.

- **Reliable deployment** to development, staging, and production.

- **Quality gates** through tests and validation.

- **Traceable releases** with logs and approvals.

Let's break this down for both GitHub Actions and Azure DevOps.

GitHub Actions for Serverless CI/CD

GitHub Actions provides a native CI/CD solution for repositories hosted on GitHub. It uses YAML files to define workflows that run on triggers like commits, pull requests, or manual dispatches.

Example: Deploying an Azure Function Using GitHub Actions

Assume you have a JavaScript or Python Azure Function in your repo with the following structure:

```
/my-function-app
  ├── host.json
  ├── function.json
  ├── index.js
  └── .github
      └── workflows
          └── deploy.yml
```

Create a `.github/workflows/deploy.yml` file:

```yaml
name: Deploy Azure Function App

on:
  push:
    branches:
      - main

jobs:
  build-and-deploy:
    runs-on: ubuntu-latest

    steps:
      - name: Checkout code
```

```
      uses: actions/checkout@v3

   - name: Set up Node.js
     uses: actions/setup-node@v3
     with:
        node-version: '18'

   - name: Install dependencies
     run: npm install

   - name: Azure Login
     uses: azure/login@v1
     with:
        creds: ${{ secrets.AZURE_CREDENTIALS }}

   - name: Deploy Function App
     uses: Azure/functions-action@v1
     with:
        app-name: 'my-function-app'
        package: '.'
```

In this example:

- `AZURE_CREDENTIALS` is a secret in your GitHub repository.

- The deployment uses the official Azure Functions GitHub Action.

To generate credentials, use the Azure CLI:

```
az ad sp create-for-rbac --name "github-actions-deploy" \
  --role contributor \
  --scopes /subscriptions/<subscription-
id>/resourceGroups/<resource-group> \
  --sdk-auth
```

Copy the output and add it as a secret named `AZURE_CREDENTIALS`.

Logic App Deployment via GitHub Actions

Deploying Logic Apps (Standard or Consumption) involves using ARM templates or Bicep files.

Example snippet to deploy a Logic App using a Bicep file:

```
- name: Deploy Logic App
  run: |
    az deployment group create \
      --resource-group ${{ secrets.RESOURCE_GROUP }} \
      --template-file infrastructure/logicapp.bicep \
      --parameters logicAppName=my-logic-app
```

You can parameterize this using GitHub secrets and workflow inputs for dynamic deployment.

Azure DevOps Pipelines for Serverless

Azure DevOps offers an enterprise-grade CI/CD service tightly integrated with the Azure ecosystem. Pipelines are defined using YAML or classic GUI editors and support robust controls like approval gates, environments, and artifact management.

Example: Azure Function CI/CD Using YAML Pipeline

Create a `azure-pipelines.yml` file in your repo:

```
trigger:
  branches:
    include:
      - main

pool:
  vmImage: 'ubuntu-latest'

variables:
  azureSubscription: 'AzureServiceConnection'
  functionAppName: 'my-function-app'
  resourceGroupName: 'my-rg'

stages:
  - stage: Build
    jobs:
      - job: BuildFunctionApp
```

```
        steps:
          - task: UseNode@2
            inputs:
              version: '18.x'
          - checkout: self
          - script: |
              npm install
            displayName: 'Install dependencies'
          - task: ArchiveFiles@2
            inputs:
              rootFolderOrFile: '.'
              includeRootFolder: false
              archiveType: 'zip'
              archiveFile:
'$(Build.ArtifactStagingDirectory)/app.zip'

          - publish: '$(Build.ArtifactStagingDirectory)/app.zip'
            artifact: functionapp

  - stage: Deploy
    dependsOn: Build
    jobs:
      - deployment: DeployFunctionApp
        environment: 'production'
        strategy:
          runOnce:
            deploy:
              steps:
                - download: current
                  artifact: functionapp

                - task: AzureWebApp@1
                  inputs:
                    azureSubscription: $(azureSubscription)
                    appType: functionApp
                    appName: $(functionAppName)
                    package:
$(Pipeline.Workspace)/functionapp/app.zip
```

Ensure your Azure Service Connection is set up in Azure DevOps under **Project Settings > Service Connections**.

Logic App Deployment in Azure DevOps

For Logic Apps, deployment is handled using ARM or Bicep templates and the Azure CLI task:

```
- task: AzureCLI@2
  inputs:
    azureSubscription: 'AzureServiceConnection'
    scriptType: 'bash'
    scriptLocation: 'inlineScript'
    inlineScript: |
      az deployment group create \
        --resource-group $(resourceGroupName) \
        --template-file infrastructure/logicapp.bicep \
        --parameters logicAppName=my-logic-app
```

Environment Promotion and Approval Gates

Both GitHub and Azure DevOps support multi-stage pipelines with environment promotion:

- **Staging → Production** flows.

- Manual or automatic approvals.

- Auditing and deployment logs.

In Azure DevOps, you can define environments with approval gates and role-based access. In GitHub, environments can have required reviewers and protection rules.

```
environment:
  name: production
  url: https://myapp.azurewebsites.net
```

This helps ensure safe, verified deployments especially in regulated or enterprise settings.

Testing in the Pipeline

CI/CD is not just about deployment—it should validate the quality of your code. Common tests include:

- **Unit tests**: Run via Jest, Mocha, PyTest, etc.

- **Integration tests**: Check connectivity and outputs.

- **Linting**: ESLint, Flake8, or custom rules.

- **Contract tests**: For APIs and event-driven flows.

- **Security scanning**: Use tools like Snyk or GitHub's CodeQL.

Example GitHub step for running tests:

```
- name: Run Tests
  run: npm test
```

Secrets and Secure Deployments

Never hardcode secrets. Instead:

- Use GitHub Secrets or Azure Key Vault.

- Set secrets as environment variables or inject at runtime.

- Rotate credentials regularly.

- Apply least privilege access to deployment service principals.

Example to inject secrets into a GitHub workflow:

```
env:
  STORAGE_KEY: ${{ secrets.STORAGE_KEY }}
```

Observability and Rollbacks

Once deployed, you need visibility into the behavior of your serverless apps.

- Integrate Application Insights and Azure Monitor into your pipeline.

- Enable logging and alerts for function errors or latency issues.

- Consider deploying in *canary* or *blue-green* patterns for safer rollouts.

Rollback strategies include:

- Redeploying the previous artifact.

- Using deployment slots (supported in Premium Plans).

- Versioning Logic Apps and Functions.

Summary and Recommendations

Setting up CI/CD pipelines for serverless applications on Azure is essential for scalable and secure software delivery. Whether you use GitHub Actions for simplicity and tight GitHub integration or Azure DevOps for enterprise workflows and controls, the benefits include:

- Reliable, consistent deployments.

- Faster feedback loops via testing.

- Secure and traceable release management.

- Support for environment promotion and rollback.

Best Practices:

- Modularize your pipeline steps (build, test, deploy).

- Integrate IaC into the same pipeline or use separate infra pipelines.

- Use secrets management consistently and securely.

- Include robust test coverage and quality gates.

- Monitor and log everything.

Adopting CI/CD transforms serverless development from an ad hoc process into a disciplined engineering practice that supports continuous innovation and operational excellence.

Deployment Strategies and Version Management

Serverless applications often power critical workloads and customer-facing experiences, making their deployment and versioning strategies pivotal to maintaining stability, delivering new features, and responding quickly to issues. Unlike traditional monolithic systems, serverless apps are composed of many small, independently deployable components—such as Azure Functions and Logic Apps—that must be coordinated and maintained effectively.

This section provides a comprehensive guide to modern deployment strategies and version control techniques tailored for Azure's serverless ecosystem. It includes practices for minimizing downtime, managing feature rollouts, isolating failures, and maintaining visibility across versions in production.

Key Considerations for Serverless Deployments

Deploying serverless applications introduces unique challenges:

- **Cold starts and latency**: New deployments may briefly increase cold start frequency.

- **Dependency management**: Serverless functions often rely on external packages or APIs.

- **Concurrency and scale**: Deployments may affect functions already running at scale.

- **State management**: Stateless designs help, but integrations (e.g., with Durable Functions) can complicate versioning.

- **Observability**: Without traditional infrastructure, monitoring and logging become even more essential.

To overcome these challenges, a combination of deployment strategies and robust versioning practices must be used.

Blue-Green Deployments

Blue-Green deployment is a strategy where two identical environments (Blue and Green) are maintained. One serves live traffic (say, Blue), while the other (Green) is updated with the new version. After testing the Green environment, traffic is switched over.

Benefits:

- Zero-downtime deployment

- Instant rollback capability

- Safe validation in a production-like environment

Implementation on Azure:

Azure Functions on a Premium Plan or App Service Plan can use **Deployment Slots**.

Steps:

1. Create a slot called staging.

2. Deploy your new version to staging.

3. Validate functionality.

4. Swap staging with production.

```
az functionapp deployment slot create \
  --name my-function-app \
  --resource-group my-rg \
  --slot staging

az functionapp deployment source config-zip \
  --src ./my-function.zip \
  --name my-function-app \
  --resource-group my-rg \
  --slot staging

az functionapp deployment slot swap \
  --name my-function-app \
  --resource-group my-rg \
  --slot staging
```

This process reduces risk and makes rollback as simple as another swap.

Canary Releases

Canary deployments release the new version to a small subset of users before a full rollout. This helps catch issues early without affecting all users.

Azure Front Door or Application Gateway can be used to manage traffic splitting between versions of your serverless application, especially if routed through HTTP endpoints.

Example: Send 10% of traffic to the new version hosted on a staging slot:

- Route 90% to `my-function-app.azurewebsites.net`

- Route 10% to `my-function-app-staging.azurewebsites.net`

You can gradually increase traffic to the canary until full confidence is achieved.

Best practices:

- Automate health checks and monitoring during the release window.

- Define clear metrics for success/failure.

- Ensure feature flags are in place for rapid deactivation if needed.

Feature Flags

Feature flags enable or disable functionality at runtime without deploying new code. They are essential in serverless for:

- Gradual rollouts

- A/B testing

- Safe rollbacks

Azure App Configuration provides native support for feature flags.

Sample: Using Feature Flags in Azure Functions

```
const appConfig = require('azure-appconfiguration');
const client =
appConfig.fromConnectionString(process.env.APP_CONFIG_CONNECTION);

const flagValue = await client.getConfigurationSetting({ key:
'NewFeatureEnabled' });

if (flagValue.value === 'true') {
  // Execute new feature logic
```

```
} else {
  // Fallback to old behavior
}
```

Flags can be toggled in the Azure portal or via CLI, instantly affecting live applications.

```
az appconfig feature set \
  --feature 'NewFeatureEnabled' \
  --name 'my-appconfig-store'
```

Versioning Azure Functions

Each deployment of a Function App effectively overwrites the previous one unless handled intentionally. There are multiple strategies to manage versions of your functions:

1. Multiple Function Apps

Create separate Function Apps for major versions (e.g., `my-func-v1`, `my-func-v2`). Each runs independently with isolated configurations and endpoints.

- **Pros**: Total isolation, independent scaling

- **Cons**: More resources used, more complex routing

2. Versioned Routes or Endpoints

Prefix your routes or function names with version identifiers.

```
[FunctionName("GetUserV1")]
[Route("v1/user/{id}")]

[FunctionName("GetUserV2")]
[Route("v2/user/{id}")]
```

This approach allows both versions to run simultaneously, offering a smoother transition.

3. Deployment Slots as Version Containers

Use deployment slots not only for staging but also to host different versions of the app. This works well when combined with traffic splitting.

Logic Apps: Versioning and Deployment Strategies

For **Logic Apps (Standard)**, versioning is often handled by:

- Exporting ARM or Bicep templates with version metadata.

- Naming workflows with version suffixes (`ProcessOrderV1`, `ProcessOrderV2`).

- Using deployment automation to manage version updates.

- Leveraging source control to track and revert versions.

For **Logic Apps (Consumption)**, built-in versioning is limited. You can simulate it by:

- Cloning existing workflows and versioning them manually.

- Routing requests via API Management or Application Gateway based on version headers.

Handling Backward Compatibility

In serverless applications where multiple clients or integrations consume APIs and workflows, backward compatibility is key.

Strategies:

- Use semantic versioning in URLs or payloads.

- Never remove or rename fields; deprecate with warnings first.

- Maintain older workflows or functions as long as clients rely on them.

- Log version usage to determine deprecation timelines.

Example: Semantic versioning in Function App route binding.

```
[FunctionName("CreateOrder")]
[Route("api/v2/orders")]
```

Monitoring Deployments

Every deployment should be accompanied by:

- **Logs** of what changed and why.

- **Telemetry**: via Application Insights or Azure Monitor.

- **Alerting**: for errors, latency spikes, and unusual behavior.

- **Dashboards**: showing version-specific metrics and traffic.

Azure Functions and Logic Apps integrate with Azure Monitor. Ensure `APPINSIGHTS_INSTRUMENTATIONKEY` is set in your environment variables.

Example to enable logging in Bicep:

```
resource appInsights 'Microsoft.Insights/components@2020-02-02' = {
  name: 'my-appinsights'
  location: location
  kind: 'web'
  properties: {
    Application_Type: 'web'
  }
}
```

Rollback Strategies

Even with the best practices, things can go wrong. Rollback planning is essential:

- Use **deployment slots** to rollback by swapping back.

- Retain previous **artifact versions** in CI/CD pipelines.

- Use **tags** or **release labels** in your repository to mark known-good states.

- For Logic Apps, export previous templates and re-deploy them on failure.

- Use **feature flags** to disable newly released functionality quickly.

GitHub and Azure DevOps both support releasing from older builds or tags, allowing easy rollback.

Summary and Recommendations

Deployment and version management are critical for delivering stable, scalable serverless solutions. While serverless platforms abstract infrastructure, they demand careful coordination to ensure smooth deployments and reliable service.

Key takeaways:

- Use **deployment slots** for zero-downtime releases.

- Adopt **canary and blue-green** strategies for safe rollout.

- Leverage **feature flags** to control functionality dynamically.

- Maintain multiple **function versions** when breaking changes are introduced.

- Monitor deployments with **telemetry** and **alerting**.

- Plan and automate **rollback** procedures for rapid recovery.

When these practices are combined with IaC and CI/CD pipelines, your serverless deployment process becomes a robust, resilient system that supports agility without sacrificing reliability.

Chapter 7: Security and Governance

Identity and Access Management

Securing serverless applications requires a robust and well-thought-out Identity and Access Management (IAM) strategy. In the cloud, especially with Azure's serverless services, IAM determines who can access your resources, what they can do, and how their actions are audited. With the abstraction that serverless provides, developers are often distanced from traditional infrastructure-level controls—making identity-centric security even more critical.

This section explores how Azure's identity platform integrates with serverless technologies like Azure Functions, Logic Apps, Event Grid, and Service Bus. It covers authentication, authorization, role-based access control (RBAC), managed identities, and best practices to ensure secure and governed access to resources.

Understanding Azure IAM Fundamentals

Azure's IAM model is based on three core principles:

- **Authentication**: Verifying who the user or service is.

- **Authorization**: Determining what they are allowed to do.

- **Auditing**: Logging and reviewing actions for compliance.

IAM in Azure is enforced through a combination of **Azure Active Directory (AAD)**, **Role-Based Access Control (RBAC)**, **resource-level permissions**, and **identity federation** for external systems.

Azure AD Integration with Serverless

Azure Active Directory (AAD) is the backbone of identity in Azure. It allows secure identity management for:

- Users (developers, administrators)

- Applications (web, mobile, desktop)

- Services (Functions, Logic Apps, etc.)

AAD supports various forms of authentication, including:

- OAuth2.0 / OpenID Connect

- SAML

- Managed identities (for apps)

- External identities (social accounts, B2B partners)

Scenario: Protecting an Azure Function with AAD

Azure Functions can require callers to authenticate using Azure AD. This is often used in APIs exposed to internal or external consumers.

To secure a function:

1. Set the authentication level to `Function` or `Anonymous` (to allow external control).

2. Enable **AAD Authentication** from the **Authentication** blade in the Azure portal.

3. Register your application in Azure AD.

4. Assign roles and scopes using the App Registrations panel.

Example configuration in `host.json`:

```
{
  "extensions": {
    "http": {
      "routePrefix": "api",
      "maxOutstandingRequests": 200,
      "maxConcurrentRequests": 100
    }
  }
}
```

Once authentication is enabled, you can validate tokens in your function code:

```
module.exports = async function (context, req) {
  const user = req.headers['x-ms-client-principal'];
  if (!user) {
    context.res = {
      status: 401,
      body: 'Unauthorized'
```

```
  };
  return;
}

context.res = {
  status: 200,
  body: `Hello, ${JSON.parse(Buffer.from(user,
'base64').toString()).userDetails}`
};
};
```

Role-Based Access Control (RBAC)

RBAC allows fine-grained access management to Azure resources. Permissions are defined through roles, which are assigned to users, groups, or service principals at various scopes:

- **Subscription**

- **Resource Group**

- **Resource (Function App, Storage, etc.)**

Common Built-in Roles:

- **Reader**: Can view resources but not make changes.

- **Contributor**: Can create and manage all types of Azure resources but cannot grant access.

- **Owner**: Full control, including permissions.

- **Function App Contributor**: Manage function apps only.

To assign a role:

```
az role assignment create \
  --assignee <principal-id> \
  --role "Function App Contributor" \
  --scope /subscriptions/<sub-id>/resourceGroups/<rg-
name>/providers/Microsoft.Web/sites/<app-name>
```

Custom roles can be created when built-in ones do not meet specific needs.

Securing Logic Apps with Identity

Logic Apps can interact with a range of services and APIs. Depending on whether you're using **Standard** or **Consumption** Logic Apps, you can configure:

- **AAD Auth for inbound requests**

- **Service connections with OAuth tokens**

- **Managed identities for API calls**

Example: Using OAuth with Logic Apps

When calling a protected Azure Function, configure the HTTP action like so:

- Method: `POST`

- URI: `https://myapp.azurewebsites.net/api/endpoint`

- Authentication:

    - Type: `OAuth 2.0`

    - Identity Provider: `Azure Active Directory`

    - Resource: `https://myapp.azurewebsites.net`

This setup requires the Logic App to have an enterprise application registered in AAD.

Managed Identities

Managed Identities eliminate the need to manage credentials in your application code. Azure automatically provisions an identity for your Function App or Logic App, allowing it to authenticate securely with other Azure services.

There are two types:

- **System-assigned**: Tied to a single resource.

- **User-assigned**: Can be shared across multiple resources.

To enable:

```
az functionapp identity assign \
  --name my-function-app \
  --resource-group my-rg
```

Then grant access to a Key Vault:

```
az keyvault set-policy \
  --name my-vault \
  --object-id <function-app-principal-id> \
  --secret-permissions get
```

In your code, access the secret:

```
import os
from azure.identity import DefaultAzureCredential
from azure.keyvault.secrets import SecretClient

credential = DefaultAzureCredential()
client = SecretClient(vault_url="https://my-vault.vault.azure.net",
credential=credential)
secret = client.get_secret("DbConnectionString")
```

This approach removes hardcoded secrets from code and config files.

Token-Based Access and Permissions

Many serverless workflows interact with APIs that require tokens. Azure AD provides access tokens through:

- **Client Credentials Flow** (app-to-app)

- **Authorization Code Flow** (user interactive)

- **On-behalf-of Flow** (delegated token passing)

For example, a Logic App calling Microsoft Graph might obtain a token via a service principal and pass it as a header:

```
GET https://graph.microsoft.com/v1.0/users
Authorization: Bearer eyJ0eXAiOiJKV1Qi...
```

You can also retrieve tokens in Azure Functions using `ManagedIdentityCredential` from the Azure SDK.

Governance with Azure Policy and Blueprints

Security is not only about access—it's also about **ensuring compliance and control**. Azure Policy allows you to enforce governance by defining conditions that resources must meet.

Examples:

- Enforce that only approved locations are used.

- Prevent creation of untagged resources.

- Require diagnostic logs to be enabled.

```
az policy assignment create \
  --policy "require-tag" \
  --scope /subscriptions/<sub-id> \
  --params '{"tagName":{"value":"Environment"}}'
```

Azure Blueprints allow bundling policies, RBAC assignments, ARM templates, and resource groups into repeatable templates for secure environments.

Logging and Auditing Access

Azure provides comprehensive logging tools for IAM events:

- **Azure Activity Logs**: Track changes in RBAC assignments.

- **Azure AD Sign-In Logs**: Monitor user and app sign-ins.

- **Diagnostic Logs**: Enable per resource (e.g., Function App logs).

Always enable logging to a **central Log Analytics workspace** or **Storage Account** for review and compliance.

```
az monitor diagnostic-settings create \
  --name 'send-logs-to-law' \
  --resource <resource-id> \
  --workspace <log-analytics-id> \
  --logs '[{"category":"AuditLogs","enabled":true}]'
```

These logs help with forensic analysis, compliance audits, and anomaly detection.

Security Best Practices

- **Use least privilege**: Always assign the minimal required role.

- **Use managed identities**: Avoid secrets in code.

- **Centralize identity**: Prefer AAD over external auth providers.

- **Monitor and alert**: Set alerts for unauthorized access attempts.

- **Tag everything**: Enforce tagging for ownership and cost tracking.

- **Isolate environments**: Separate dev, test, and prod with role boundaries.

Summary and Recommendations

Securing your serverless architecture starts with identity. Azure's IAM tools—from Azure AD to RBAC and Managed Identities—provide the framework to control access at every level of your application stack.

Checklist:

- ✓ Protect serverless endpoints with AAD.

- ✓ Use RBAC to control access to Function Apps and Logic Apps.

- ✓ Replace credentials with Managed Identities.

- ✓ Secure external API calls with OAuth and token flows.

- ✓ Audit and log all access and changes.

- ✓ Automate security enforcement using Azure Policy.

When properly configured, identity becomes your strongest security boundary—one that scales with your serverless app and evolves with your organization's needs.

Using Managed Identities and Key Vault

Managing credentials, secrets, and authentication tokens securely is one of the most critical aspects of building serverless applications on Azure. Traditional approaches—such as storing API keys in configuration files or environment variables—are prone to leaks, difficult to audit, and challenging to rotate. Azure addresses this with **Managed Identities** and **Azure Key Vault**, enabling you to secure your serverless applications without embedding secrets in code or deployment pipelines.

This section explains how Managed Identities work, how to use them effectively within Azure Functions and Logic Apps, and how to integrate them with Azure Key Vault to securely access secrets, connection strings, certificates, and other sensitive data.

Introduction to Managed Identities

Managed Identities are system-assigned or user-assigned identities provided by Azure Active Directory (Azure AD). These identities allow your applications and services to authenticate to any Azure AD-supported service, like Key Vault or Azure Storage, without needing to manage credentials manually.

There are two types:

- **System-assigned managed identity**: Automatically created and tied to a single resource (e.g., a Function App). Deleted when the resource is deleted.

- **User-assigned managed identity**: A standalone Azure resource that can be shared across multiple services.

Benefits include:

- No credentials stored in code or configuration

- Automatic token management

- Tight integration with Azure RBAC and Key Vault

Enabling Managed Identity in Azure Functions

To enable a **system-assigned managed identity** for an Azure Function:

Azure CLI

```
az functionapp identity assign \
  --name my-function-app \
  --resource-group my-resource-group
```

After running this, your Function App will have an identity represented by a service principal in Azure AD. You can view the identity's object ID in the portal or via CLI.

Accessing Azure Key Vault from Azure Functions

Once your Function App has a managed identity, you can use it to read secrets from Azure Key Vault securely.

Step 1: Create a Key Vault and Add a Secret

```
az keyvault create --name my-keyvault --resource-group my-resource-group

az keyvault secret set --vault-name my-keyvault \
  --name "DbConnectionString" \
  --value "Server=mydb;Database=appdb;User
Id=appuser;Password=securepwd;"
```

Step 2: Grant Access to the Managed Identity

```
az keyvault set-policy \
  --name my-keyvault \
  --object-id <identity-object-id> \
  --secret-permissions get
```

Step 3: Access Secret in Code (Python Example)

```
from azure.identity import DefaultAzureCredential
from azure.keyvault.secrets import SecretClient
```

```
credential = DefaultAzureCredential()
vault_url = "https://my-keyvault.vault.azure.net"
client = SecretClient(vault_url=vault_url, credential=credential)

secret = client.get_secret("DbConnectionString")
print("Database connection string:", secret.value)
```

`DefaultAzureCredential` automatically uses the Function App's managed identity when deployed in Azure.

In local development, it falls back to your Azure CLI or Visual Studio credentials.

Accessing Azure Key Vault in Node.js Azure Function

```
const { DefaultAzureCredential } = require("@azure/identity");
const { SecretClient } = require("@azure/keyvault-secrets");

module.exports = async function (context, req) {
  const credential = new DefaultAzureCredential();
  const vaultName = "my-keyvault";
  const url = `https://${vaultName}.vault.azure.net`;
  const client = new SecretClient(url, credential);

  const secret = await client.getSecret("DbConnectionString");

  context.res = {
    status: 200,
    body: `The secret is: ${secret.value}`
  };
};
```

Add the following environment variable in Azure Configuration:

```
AZURE_CLIENT_ID=<your-managed-identity-client-id>
```

Although this is optional for system-assigned identities, it may be required for user-assigned identities.

Using Managed Identities in Logic Apps (Standard)

Logic Apps (Standard) support Managed Identities for actions like HTTP, Azure Functions, Key Vault access, and more.

Enabling Managed Identity

1. Go to your Logic App in the Azure Portal.

2. Navigate to **Identity** > **System assigned** > **Enable**.

3. Save changes.

Grant Key Vault Access

```
az keyvault set-policy \
  --name my-keyvault \
  --object-id <logic-app-identity-object-id> \
  --secret-permissions get
```

Access Secret Using Managed Identity

Within your Logic App, add an **HTTP action**:

- **Method**: GET

- **URI**: `https://<keyvault-name>.vault.azure.net/secrets/DbConnectionString?api-version=7.2`

- **Authentication**:

    - **Type**: `Managed Identity`

    - **Identity**: `System-assigned managed identity`

    - **Audience**: `https://vault.azure.net`

The secret is returned as JSON and can be parsed using `@json()` or `@body()` expressions.

Using Key Vault for Application Settings

You can link Function App settings directly to Key Vault:

1. Navigate to **Configuration** in your Function App.

2. Add a new setting like DbConnectionString.

3. Set its value to:

```
@Microsoft.KeyVault(SecretUri=https://my-
keyvault.vault.azure.net/secrets/DbConnectionString/)
```

Make sure the Function App has get permissions on the Key Vault. Azure resolves the secret at runtime and injects it as an environment variable.

This method works across all Azure App Services including Web Apps, APIs, and Functions.

User-Assigned Managed Identities

Use this when you want multiple services to share the same identity (e.g., staging and production apps with shared access policies).

Create a User-Assigned Identity

```
az identity create \
  --name shared-identity \
  --resource-group my-resource-group
```

Assign to Azure Function

```
az functionapp identity assign \
  --name my-function-app \
  --resource-group my-resource-group \
  --identities /subscriptions/<sub-id>/resourceGroups/<rg-name>/providers/Microsoft.ManagedIdentity/userAssignedIdentities/shared-identity
```

You can now grant this identity access to Key Vault, Storage, or any Azure service.

Best Practices for Secure Identity and Secret Management

1. **Avoid hardcoded secrets**: Never store secrets in code or config files.

2. **Use managed identities**: For all serverless and app service resources.

3. **Limit permissions**: Use least-privilege access in Key Vault and other services.

4. **Audit access**: Enable Key Vault diagnostics and monitor secret access logs.

5. **Rotate secrets**: Automate secret rotation and use event-driven triggers for refresh.

6. **Separate secrets per environment**: Avoid sharing secrets across environments.

7. **Use custom roles and policies**: For granular control over resource access.

Monitoring and Auditing with Azure Monitor

Key Vault logs every access and action. You can route logs to:

- **Log Analytics**

- **Event Hubs**

- **Storage Accounts**

Enable diagnostics via CLI:

```
az monitor diagnostic-settings create \
  --resource /subscriptions/<sub-id>/resourceGroups/<rg-
name>/providers/Microsoft.KeyVault/vaults/my-keyvault \
  --workspace <log-analytics-workspace-id> \
  --logs '[{"category":"AuditEvent","enabled":true}]'
```

Use **Azure Monitor Workbooks** to visualize access patterns, failed access attempts, and frequency of usage.

Summary and Recommendations

The combination of **Managed Identities** and **Azure Key Vault** is a best-in-class solution for securing credentials and secrets in serverless apps. It supports dynamic, secure, and fully auditable access patterns while removing the burden of secret management from developers.

Quick Recap:

- ✓ Use **Managed Identity** in every Function App and Logic App.

- ✓ Store **secrets, keys, and certs** in Azure Key Vault.

- ✓ Grant only the necessary permissions using `az keyvault set-policy`.

- ✓ Read secrets in code using Azure SDKs with `DefaultAzureCredential`.

- ✓ Enable logging for auditing and compliance.

- ✓ Prefer **user-assigned identities** for shared access scenarios.

Implementing these practices ensures your applications are secure, compliant, and future-proof as your infrastructure scales.

Monitoring, Auditing, and Compliance Tools

Security is not only about controlling access—it's also about visibility, traceability, and accountability. In the serverless world, where applications are built with ephemeral infrastructure and managed services, traditional monitoring and auditing techniques fall short. Azure provides a rich set of tools to track, log, audit, and ensure compliance across your serverless workloads.

This section explores the tools, configurations, and best practices for implementing end-to-end observability in serverless applications. We'll cover key services like **Azure Monitor**, **Application Insights**, **Log Analytics**, **Azure Policy**, **Activity Logs**, and **Microsoft Defender for Cloud**, all with a focus on Azure Functions, Logic Apps, and other serverless resources.

The Importance of Monitoring and Auditing in Serverless

Key reasons why observability is crucial for serverless apps:

- **Short-lived execution**: Functions may only run for milliseconds, making real-time and historical logging vital.

- **Complex integrations**: Logic Apps and Functions often connect to databases, APIs, queues, and other services.

- **Security and compliance requirements**: Regulations like GDPR, HIPAA, and SOC demand audit trails and data protection.

- **Operational efficiency**: Without insights into failures or latency, diagnosing issues becomes extremely difficult.

Azure's monitoring and compliance ecosystem is designed to provide this visibility out-of-the-box—if configured properly.

Azure Monitor Overview

Azure Monitor is the central service for collecting, analyzing, and acting on telemetry from your Azure and hybrid environments. It includes:

- **Metrics**: Numerical data over time (CPU usage, execution count)

- **Logs**: Text-based data for tracing, diagnostics, and auditing

- **Alerts**: Triggered based on metrics, logs, or activity

- **Workbooks**: Interactive reports and dashboards

- **Insights**: Specialized monitoring views for different services

Azure Monitor integrates with **Application Insights** (for app-level telemetry) and **Log Analytics** (for log querying and storage).

Application Insights for Azure Functions

Application Insights is a powerful tool to monitor performance, detect anomalies, track usage, and diagnose errors in serverless apps.

Enabling Application Insights

When creating a Function App via portal or CLI, you can link an Application Insights resource.

```
az functionapp create \
  --name my-function-app \
  --resource-group my-rg \
  --storage-account mystorage \
  --plan my-plan \
  --app-insights my-insights
```

Or configure it later via the Azure Portal under **Settings > Application Insights**.

Telemetry Collected by Default

Once integrated, Application Insights captures:

- **Request telemetry**: URL, duration, success/failure

- **Dependencies**: Calls to databases, APIs

- **Exceptions**: Errors with stack traces

- **Custom Events**: User-defined logs

- **Performance counters**

Example of custom logging:

```
var telemetry = new TelemetryClient();
telemetry.TrackEvent("NewOrderReceived", new Dictionary<string,
string>
{
    { "CustomerId", "12345" },
    { "OrderAmount", "79.99" }
});
```

Or in JavaScript:

```
const appInsights = require("applicationinsights");
appInsights.setup().start();
const client = appInsights.defaultClient;

client.trackEvent({ name: "OrderSubmitted", properties: { userId:
"abc123" } });
```

Monitoring Logic Apps

Logic Apps also emit telemetry to Azure Monitor. For **Logic Apps (Standard)**, you can connect Application Insights explicitly in the `host.json` file:

```
{
```

```
"logging": {
  "applicationInsights": {
    "samplingSettings": {
      "isEnabled": true
    }
  }
}
}
```

For **Logic Apps (Consumption)**, logs are available in:

- **Run History**: Step-by-step logs per execution

- **Azure Monitor Logs**: When diagnostics are enabled

- **Log Analytics workspace**

Enabling Diagnostics Logs

```
az monitor diagnostic-settings create \
  --resource "/subscriptions/<sub-
id>/resourceGroups/<rg>/providers/Microsoft.Logic/workflows/my-
logic-app" \
  --workspace <workspace-id> \
  --logs '[{"category":"WorkflowRuntime","enabled":true}]'
```

This enables access to historical logs and centralized dashboards.

Azure Activity Logs and Audit Trail

Azure Activity Logs provide insight into operations at the management layer (e.g., deployment, resource creation, RBAC changes). It is critical for:

- **Security audits**

- **Change tracking**

- **Governance enforcement**

Activity Logs are automatically available in Azure but should be routed to **Log Analytics**, **Event Hubs**, or **Storage** for long-term retention.

Example: Routing to Log Analytics

```
az monitor diagnostic-settings create \
  --name "activity-logs" \
  --resource "/providers/Microsoft.Resources/subscriptions/<sub-id>"
\
  --workspace <workspace-id> \
  --logs '[{"category":"Administrative","enabled":true}]'
```

Use **Log Analytics** to query actions:

```
AzureActivity
| where ResourceProvider == "Microsoft.Web"
| where OperationNameValue contains "write"
| project TimeGenerated, OperationNameValue, Caller, Resource,
Status
```

Azure Policy for Compliance Enforcement

Azure Policy is a governance tool that lets you define rules and effects over your resources. It can:

- Deny or audit insecure configurations

- Enforce tagging and location rules

- Require diagnostic logging

- Validate resource naming conventions

Sample Policy: Enforce Application Insights on Functions

```
{
  "if": {
    "allOf": [
      {
        "field": "type",
        "equals": "Microsoft.Web/sites"
      },
      {
        "field": "kind",
        "contains": "functionapp"
      },
```

```
    {
      "not": {
        "field":
"Microsoft.Web/sites/siteConfig.appInsightsEnabled",
        "equals": "true"
      }
    }
  ]
},
"then": {
  "effect": "deny"
}
}
```

Assign this policy at the subscription level to enforce consistency across teams.

Microsoft Defender for Cloud

Defender for Cloud is a built-in tool for continuous security assessment and threat protection across Azure services. For serverless applications, it helps with:

- Identifying insecure configurations (e.g., missing App Insights, no encryption)

- Suggesting RBAC hardening

- Alerting on unusual behavior (e.g., suspicious HTTP requests)

- Integration with SIEM tools like Microsoft Sentinel

Enable it via:

```
az security auto-provisioning-setting update --name default --auto-provision "On"
```

You'll start receiving security recommendations and alerts for services including:

- Function Apps

- Logic Apps

- Key Vault

- Storage and Cosmos DB

Alerts and Automation

Set up alerts to trigger based on metrics or logs:

Create Alert for Failed Azure Function Executions

```
az monitor metrics alert create \
  --name "FunctionFailureAlert" \
  --resource-group my-rg \
  --scopes /subscriptions/<sub-
id>/resourceGroups/<rg>/providers/Microsoft.Web/sites/my-func \
  --condition "totalRequests > 10 where ResultType == 'Failure'" \
  --description "Alert when function failures spike"
```

Alerts can trigger:

- Email notifications

- SMS or push via Azure app

- Webhooks

- Logic Apps for automated responses

Workbooks and Dashboards

Azure Workbooks offer highly customizable and interactive dashboards to visualize metrics and logs. These are ideal for:

- SLA reporting

- Security posture overviews

- Custom telemetry visualizations

- Environment-specific monitoring

Use templates or build your own with Kusto queries. For example, to show error trends over time:

```
AppTraces
| where SeverityLevel >= 3
| summarize Count=count() by bin(TimeGenerated, 1h)
```

Summary and Recommendations

Effective monitoring, auditing, and compliance are essential for maintaining secure, stable, and scalable serverless applications. Azure offers an integrated ecosystem that, when configured correctly, provides deep visibility, automatic alerts, and policy enforcement across your entire workload.

Checklist:

- ✓ Enable Application Insights for all Function Apps and Logic Apps.

- ✓ Route diagnostic logs to a centralized Log Analytics workspace.

- ✓ Configure Azure Policy to enforce compliance and secure configurations.

- ✓ Use Activity Logs and Log Analytics to audit changes and access.

- ✓ Set up actionable alerts and automated workflows for critical events.

- ✓ Enable Microsoft Defender for Cloud for continuous security posture management.

- ✓ Build dashboards using Azure Workbooks for team-wide visibility.

By making observability a first-class citizen in your serverless architecture, you not only detect issues early but also maintain trust, meet compliance requirements, and continuously improve your cloud operations.

Chapter 8: Performance Optimization and Cost Management

Monitoring and Diagnostics with Azure Monitor

Optimizing the performance of serverless applications in Azure requires a deep understanding of how resources behave in production, how workloads scale, and how to track down and resolve performance bottlenecks. Azure Monitor is the cornerstone of observability within the Azure ecosystem and provides a comprehensive platform for collecting, analyzing, and acting on telemetry from your applications and infrastructure. This section will explore in detail how you can use Azure Monitor to gain deep insights into your serverless workloads and make informed decisions to optimize performance and control costs.

Introduction to Azure Monitor

Azure Monitor is a platform service that provides full-stack monitoring for applications, infrastructure, and networks in Azure. It helps developers and operations teams collect data, analyze it, and respond to performance anomalies in real time.

The core components of Azure Monitor include:

- **Metrics**: Numerical data representing performance. Examples include CPU usage, memory consumption, and function execution count.

- **Logs**: Event and trace data that provide contextual information about operations and failures.

- **Alerts**: Rules that trigger actions when thresholds are breached.

- **Dashboards**: Visualizations of metrics and logs for quick status updates.

- **Application Insights**: A subset of Azure Monitor focused specifically on application performance and usage analytics.

Enabling Monitoring for Azure Functions

By default, when you create a Function App, Azure enables some level of monitoring. However, to get the most out of Azure Monitor, you should explicitly integrate Application Insights.

Steps to Enable Application Insights for a Function App

1. Go to your Function App in the Azure Portal.

2. Navigate to **Settings > Application Insights**.

3. If not enabled, choose to enable Application Insights.

4. Create a new or select an existing Application Insights resource.

5. Save the configuration and allow time for telemetry to start flowing.

Once enabled, Application Insights will start collecting data such as request rates, response times, failure rates, and dependency information.

Sample Telemetry Initialization (C#)

```csharp
using Microsoft.ApplicationInsights;
using Microsoft.ApplicationInsights.Extensibility;

public static class TelemetrySetup
{
    public static TelemetryClient CreateClient()
    {
        var configuration = TelemetryConfiguration.CreateDefault();
        configuration.InstrumentationKey =
Environment.GetEnvironmentVariable("APPINSIGHTS_INSTRUMENTATIONKEY")
;

        return new TelemetryClient(configuration);
    }
}
```

You can inject this `TelemetryClient` into your Azure Functions and use it to log custom events, exceptions, or metrics.

Analyzing Metrics for Performance Bottlenecks

Metrics provide real-time visibility into the health and performance of your applications. Azure Monitor automatically collects several standard metrics for serverless services, including:

- **Function Execution Count**

- **Function Execution Time**

- **Function Errors**

- **Memory Working Set**

You can access these metrics through:

- Azure Portal

- Azure CLI

- Azure Monitor REST API

- Azure SDKs

Using Azure CLI to Query Metrics

```
az monitor metrics list \
  --resource /subscriptions/{sub-id}/resourceGroups/{rg}/providers/Microsoft.Web/sites/{functionApp} \
  --metric "FunctionExecutionUnits" \
  --interval PT1M \
  --aggregation Average
```

This command returns the average number of execution units (a proxy for compute consumption) per minute, helping you identify performance spikes.

Logs and Diagnostics with Application Insights

While metrics tell you **what** happened, logs explain **why**. Application Insights provides access to logs via Kusto Query Language (KQL), a powerful query language for analyzing telemetry data.

Sample KQL Query for Failed Requests

```
requests
| where success == false
| summarize count() by resultCode, operation_Name, bin(timestamp, 1h)
```

This query shows you the count of failed requests by HTTP status code and function name, grouped by hour. Such queries can help identify recurring issues or diagnose sudden spikes in errors.

Adding Custom Traces in JavaScript Functions

```
const appInsights = require("applicationinsights");
appInsights.setup(process.env.APPINSIGHTS_INSTRUMENTATIONKEY).start(
);
const client = appInsights.defaultClient;
```

```
module.exports = async function (context, req) {
    client.trackTrace({ message: "Function triggered", severity: 1
});
    context.res = {
        body: "Hello, world"
    };
};
```

These logs will appear in Application Insights and can be filtered using KQL.

Setting Up Alerts for Proactive Monitoring

Azure Monitor alerts allow you to create rules based on metrics or logs. When a condition is met, an action group can trigger email notifications, webhook calls, Azure Functions, Logic Apps, and more.

Example: Creating an Alert for High Failure Rate

1. In Azure Monitor, go to **Alerts** and select **+ New Alert Rule**.

2. Select the Function App as the resource.

3. For the condition, use `Function Errors` with a threshold of `>` `5` in the last 5 minutes.

4. Add an action group (email, SMS, Logic App, etc.).

5. Define the alert rule name and enable it.

Visualizing Insights with Dashboards and Workbooks

Visual tools help quickly identify trends or issues. Azure Monitor offers:

- **Dashboards**: Customizable views of metrics and logs.

- **Workbooks**: Interactive reports that combine visuals, text, and queries.

Creating a Workbook for Function Performance

1. Navigate to Azure Monitor > Workbooks.

2. Create a new workbook and add a **Query** tile.

3. Use a KQL query to show average execution time by function.

```
requests
| summarize avg(duration) by operation_Name
```

4. Add visuals like bar charts or line graphs to highlight trends.

These dashboards and workbooks can be shared across your team for better collaboration and visibility.

Integrating Azure Monitor with Other Tools

Azure Monitor integrates with:

- **Azure DevOps**: Surface telemetry in release pipelines.

- **Grafana**: Use Azure Monitor plugin to visualize metrics.

- **Power BI**: Pull data for advanced analytics and reporting.

- **Event Hubs**: Stream telemetry data to external systems.

Exporting Logs to Event Hub

```
az monitor diagnostic-settings create \
  --resource {functionAppResourceId} \
  --name "export-to-eventhub" \
  --event-hub-name {eventHubName} \
  --event-hub-rule-id {eventHubRuleId} \
  --logs '[{"category": "FunctionAppLogs", "enabled": true}]'
```

This setup allows you to stream logs to external SIEM systems or custom dashboards.

Best Practices for Monitoring and Diagnostics

1. **Enable Application Insights by default** in all Function Apps.

2. **Tag telemetry** with contextual information such as user ID or request ID.

3. **Use distributed tracing** across services to follow a transaction across multiple components.

4. **Avoid excessive logging**, which can inflate costs and obscure signal-to-noise ratio.

5. **Regularly audit alert rules** and action groups to ensure relevance and effectiveness.

Summary

Monitoring and diagnostics are foundational to building reliable, high-performance serverless applications. Azure Monitor and Application Insights offer a robust suite of tools that provide deep visibility into system behavior, performance trends, and operational anomalies. By leveraging metrics, logs, alerts, and visualizations, you can proactively manage your serverless workloads, improve user experience, and optimize operational costs.

In the next section, we'll explore how to optimize cold starts and effectively manage scaling behavior in serverless applications to further boost performance.

Optimizing Cold Start and Scaling

Cold start and scaling are two critical considerations when architecting serverless applications, especially in platforms like Azure Functions. These factors directly affect performance, user experience, and ultimately, cost efficiency. A cold start refers to the delay incurred when a serverless function is invoked after being idle, while scaling deals with how the system adjusts resources in response to demand. In this section, we'll dive deep into techniques and best practices for minimizing cold start impact and ensuring smooth scaling in production workloads.

Understanding Cold Starts

When an Azure Function is triggered after a period of inactivity, the runtime environment has to initialize several components:

- The underlying compute resource (container or VM)

- Runtime environment (e.g., Node.js, .NET, Python)

- Application code and dependencies

- Configuration settings (environment variables, secrets)

This initialization process can take anywhere from a few hundred milliseconds to several seconds depending on the function's complexity, language, and hosting plan.

Cold starts can significantly degrade performance, especially for latency-sensitive applications such as real-time APIs, chatbots, or IoT systems.

Example Cold Start Scenario

An HTTP-triggered Azure Function in the Consumption Plan might exhibit the following:

- Warm invocation: 100ms

- Cold start invocation: 3,000ms+

The discrepancy in performance can frustrate users or break SLAs.

Hosting Plans and Cold Start Impact

Azure Functions offers several hosting options, each affecting cold start behavior differently.

Hosting Plan	Cold Starts	Description
Consumption Plan	Yes	Pay-per-use, auto-scaling; cold starts can occur after idle time.
Premium Plan	No (if pre-warmed)	Pre-warmed instances eliminate cold starts.
Dedicated (App Service) Plan	No	Always-on compute, no cold starts, but higher cost.

For mission-critical apps, the **Premium Plan** with pre-warmed instances is the best choice to reduce latency.

Configuring Pre-Warmed Instances (Premium Plan)

In the Azure Portal:

1. Go to your Function App.

2. Under **Settings**, choose **Scale-Out (App Service Plan)**.

3. Set **Minimum number of instances** to 1 or more.

This ensures there's always at least one initialized instance ready to handle traffic.

Techniques to Minimize Cold Starts

1. Use Premium Plan with Always-Ready Instances

As mentioned, the Premium Plan allows you to configure warm instances that are always running. This is the most effective method for eliminating cold starts entirely.

2. Reduce Dependency Loading Time

Keep your application lightweight by minimizing startup tasks such as:

- Redundant package imports

- Large dependency trees

- Synchronous blocking calls

Node.js Example: Avoid Heavy Packages at Startup

```
// Bad
const moment = require('moment'); // heavy

module.exports = async function (context, req) {
    const time = moment().format();
    context.res = { body: `Current time: ${time}` };
};

// Better
module.exports = async function (context, req) {
    const time = new Date().toISOString(); // native Date object
    context.res = { body: `Current time: ${time}` };
};
```

3. Minimize Cold Path Initialization

Avoid initializing services like databases, external APIs, or authentication providers on every request. Instead, initialize them once and reuse.

```
// Initialize once
const dbClient = createDatabaseClient();

module.exports = async function (context, req) {
    const data = await dbClient.query("SELECT * FROM items");
    context.res = { body: data };
};
```

This pattern avoids repeated setup and speeds up cold and warm starts alike.

4. Reduce Application Size

The time to load your function's package and dependencies affects cold start duration. Use tree-shaking, pruning, and smaller Docker images if deploying via containers.

In .NET projects, use PublishTrimmed:

```
dotnet publish -c Release -r win-x64 /p:PublishTrimmed=true
```

5. Warm-Up Triggers

You can configure a timer-triggered function to run every few minutes to keep the function app warm.

```
[FunctionName("WarmUp")]
public static void Run([TimerTrigger("0 */4 * * * *")] TimerInfo
myTimer, ILogger log)
{
    log.LogInformation("Keeping Function App warm.");
}
```

This simple workaround helps reduce the frequency of cold starts, though it's more of a hack than a long-term solution.

Scaling Serverless Applications

Azure Functions scale based on events and triggers. The platform monitors load and automatically adds or removes compute instances. Key factors influencing scale include:

- Trigger type (HTTP, Event Hub, Queue, etc.)
- Plan type (Consumption, Premium)
- Concurrency limits
- Throttling and quotas

Event-Driven Scaling

Azure automatically increases instances of your Function App when:

- Event queues grow
- HTTP request volume increases
- Processing time exceeds thresholds

This makes serverless ideal for bursty workloads.

Scaling Characteristics by Trigger

Trigger Type	Scaling Behavior
HTTP (via HTTP trigger)	Scales out on request rate
Event Hub	Scales based on partitions and load
Queue Storage	Scales based on queue length and age
Timer	Does not scale

Tips for Optimizing Scaling

1. Tune Concurrency Settings

Each function app instance can handle multiple executions concurrently, depending on trigger type.

For HTTP triggers, use maxConcurrentRequestsPerInstance in host.json:

```
{
  "extensions": {
    "http": {
      "maxConcurrentRequestsPerInstance": 100
    }
  }
}
```

For Event Hub triggers, concurrency depends on the number of partitions and batchSize.

```
{
  "eventHub": {
    "batchSize": 200,
    "maxBatchSize": 300
  }
}
```

2. Use Durable Functions Wisely

Durable Functions enable long-running workflows, but poor design can hurt scalability. Avoid:

- Excessive parallel fan-out

- Holding state too long

- Orchestration loops

Design orchestrations to be resilient, short-lived per step, and checkpoint frequently.

3. Set Instance and Scale-Out Limits

In the Premium Plan, you can define limits to control burstiness:

```
{
  "functionAppScaleLimit": 10
}
```

This prevents unexpected costs during traffic spikes.

4. Use Autoscale Rules (Premium/Dedicated Plans)

With autoscale rules, you can define custom logic:

- Increase instances if CPU > 70% for 5 minutes

- Decrease if below 30% for 10 minutes

Set these in the Azure Portal or via Azure Resource Manager templates.

5. Leverage Azure Load Testing

Azure Load Testing helps simulate traffic and see how your Function App scales under stress.

Run tests during development and before major releases to ensure stability and performance.

Monitoring Scaling and Cold Start Behavior

Use Application Insights to track cold start occurrences:

```
requests
| where cloud_RoleInstance contains "coldstart"
| summarize count() by bin(timestamp, 5m)
```

Alternatively, track metrics such as `FunctionExecutionUnits` and `Function Execution Count` to infer scaling patterns.

Summary

Cold start latency and scaling behavior are central to the user experience and operational efficiency of serverless applications. By understanding the different hosting models, tuning your application's startup process, and leveraging warm-up patterns and scalable architecture, you can significantly reduce cold start impact. Additionally, configuring your app to scale smoothly based on demand ensures resilience during peak loads while optimizing costs.

In the next section, we will explore cost management strategies to estimate, track, and control the financial impact of running serverless workloads at scale.

Estimating and Controlling Costs

Cost management is a foundational aspect of operating serverless applications in Azure. While serverless platforms like Azure Functions offer a "pay-per-use" billing model that can dramatically reduce overhead compared to traditional infrastructure, costs can still grow unexpectedly when workloads scale rapidly or inefficient resource usage occurs. Understanding how to estimate, monitor, and control these expenses is critical to maintaining a sustainable and optimized cloud architecture.

This section explores strategies for forecasting costs, identifying common cost drivers, utilizing Azure's built-in cost analysis tools, and implementing governance policies to ensure long-term financial control.

The Serverless Billing Model in Azure

Azure Functions and other serverless services typically follow a consumption-based pricing model. For Azure Functions in the Consumption Plan, the main billing dimensions include:

- **Execution Count**: The total number of function invocations.

- **Execution Time (GB-s)**: Based on function runtime and allocated memory.

- **Premium Features**: Pre-warmed instances and VNET integration in Premium Plans.

- **Outbound Data Transfer**: Charges apply for data leaving Azure data centers.

Azure Functions Pricing Breakdown (Consumption Plan)

Metric	Description	Example

Executions	First 1 million free/month, then $0.20/million	5 million executions = $0.80
Execution Time (GB-s)	First 400,000 GB-s/month free, then billed	512MB running 2s = 1 GB-s
Premium Plan Costs	Billed based on reserved instances	1 core, 3.5GB = ~$0.16/hr
Data Transfer	Based on volume of egress traffic	10 GB out = ~$1.30

While the free tiers cover most development and small production needs, heavy or inefficient use can rapidly increase costs.

Estimating Costs for Azure Functions

Azure provides several tools for cost estimation:

- **Azure Pricing Calculator**

- **Azure Cost Management + Billing**

- **Programmatic cost estimation via SDK or REST API**

Using the Azure Pricing Calculator

1. Visit https://azure.com/pricing/calculator

2. Add **Functions**, **Logic Apps**, or any other serverless services to your estimate.

3. Input anticipated usage:

   o Executions per month

   o Average execution duration (ms)

   o Memory allocation (MB)

4. Review the detailed cost projection.

Example Estimate for Azure Function:

- Executions: 10 million/month

- Average duration: 2 seconds

- Memory: 512 MB

Cost ≈

(10M executions * 2s * 0.5GB) = 10 million GB-s

First 400,000 GB-s are free, so 9.6M GB-s billed

Billed usage: 9.6M GB-s * $0.000016 = $153.60

Execution count: First 1M free, 9M * $0.20 = $1.80

Total ≈ $155.40/month

Controlling Costs in Production

1. Optimize Execution Time and Memory

Function runtime is a primary cost driver. You are charged for the duration multiplied by the allocated memory.

Strategies:

- Refactor code to reduce execution time.

- Use asynchronous calls and avoid blocking operations.

- Profile memory usage and reduce allocation where possible.

```
// Instead of blocking wait:
await doHeavyCalculation();

// Use parallel processing where possible:
await Promise.all([
    task1(),
    task2(),
    task3()
]);
```

2. Use Premium Plan Only When Necessary

Premium Plans offer better performance and no cold starts, but come at a fixed cost. Only use them when needed for:

- Low-latency requirements

- High concurrency

- VNET integration

Switch to the Consumption Plan for less time-sensitive or background tasks.

3. Avoid Unintended Triggers

Ensure that your functions are not unintentionally triggered at high frequencies. This is a common cost pitfall with triggers like:

- Timer triggers set too frequently

- Event Grid or Event Hub triggers with large volumes

- Queue triggers processing poison messages repeatedly

Use proper filters, conditions, and dead-letter queues to avoid unnecessary invocations.

4. Consolidate Functions When Appropriate

Functions are billed per invocation, so consolidating logic into fewer invocations can reduce cost. However, do not over-consolidate to the point of hurting maintainability.

5. Utilize Logic Apps Wisely

Logic Apps have their own cost structure based on connectors and actions. Standard Logic Apps (in the new single-tenant model) can be more cost-effective for high-volume workloads compared to the original consumption-based model.

Example cost-saving tip: Instead of using a premium connector for every single email, batch messages and send them together.

Monitoring and Analyzing Serverless Costs

Azure offers built-in tools to track and visualize cloud spending.

Azure Cost Management + Billing

Key features:

- Budget creation and alerting

- Cost by service, resource, or tag

- Forecasts and trends

- Daily and monthly views

Steps:

1. Go to **Cost Management + Billing** in Azure Portal.

2. Select your subscription.

3. View cost analysis by resource type.

4. Filter by Function Apps, Logic Apps, Event Hubs, etc.

Sample Cost Alert Rule

You can create an alert if Function App usage exceeds a budget.

1. Go to **Cost Management > Budgets**.

2. Click **+ Add** to create a new budget.

3. Set threshold (e.g., $100/month).

4. Add an action group to send an email or trigger a Logic App if exceeded.

This helps catch runaway costs early.

Programmatic Cost Monitoring

You can use Azure APIs or SDKs to access cost data programmatically. Example using Azure CLI:

```
az consumption usage list \
  --start-date 2024-04-01 \
  --end-date 2024-04-30 \
  --query "[?contains(meterDetails.meterName, 'Function
Execution')]" \
  --output table
```

Or query cost data in Azure Resource Graph:

```
Usage
| where ResourceType contains "functions"
```

```
| summarize totalCost = sum(PreTaxCost) by ResourceGroupName,
ResourceName
```

Governance and Cost Control Best Practices

1. Use Tags for Cost Attribution

Apply resource tags for environment, department, or project name. This enables more granular cost analysis.

```
az resource tag --tags Project=CustomerPortal Environment=Prod
```

Then filter cost data:

```
Usage
| where Tags["Project"] == "CustomerPortal"
```

2. Implement Policy and Budgets

Azure Policy can restrict deployments that exceed certain pricing tiers or regions. Use Azure Blueprints to standardize resource creation with cost constraints.

3. Clean Up Idle or Orphaned Resources

Regularly audit:

- Unused function apps

- Expired staging slots

- Old Logic Apps

- Event Hubs with no subscribers

Use Azure Advisor and Cost Analysis to identify underutilized services.

4. Separate Non-Production Environments

Create separate subscriptions or resource groups for dev, test, and prod. Apply separate budgets and alerts to each to prevent cross-impact.

5. Evaluate Savings Plans and Reserved Instances

For non-serverless resources or hybrid environments, Azure offers reserved instances or savings plans that can reduce long-term costs by up to 72%.

While serverless itself doesn't benefit directly, offloading parts of workloads to these resources can help.

Summary

Cost estimation and control in serverless environments are vital for sustainable and scalable operations. Azure's serverless model provides inherent efficiency through pay-per-use billing, but without proper oversight, costs can balloon due to misconfigurations, excessive invocations, or under-optimized logic.

By using the Azure Pricing Calculator, optimizing resource use, consolidating functions, and setting up robust monitoring and governance with Azure Cost Management, you can confidently operate serverless workloads at scale while maintaining financial visibility and control.

In the next chapter, we will explore how these cost optimization strategies play out in real-world enterprise solutions and high-throughput applications.

Chapter 9: Real-World Use Cases and Case Studies

Enterprise Automation Workflows

Enterprises are constantly under pressure to streamline operations, reduce manual effort, and ensure consistent execution of business processes. Serverless technologies like Azure Functions, Logic Apps, Event Grid, and Service Bus offer a highly scalable, cost-efficient, and low-maintenance way to implement automation across various departments—from finance and HR to IT operations and customer service.

In this section, we will explore how to design and implement robust enterprise automation workflows using serverless tools on Azure. We'll walk through common automation scenarios, architecture patterns, implementation strategies, and pitfalls to avoid, with code examples where applicable.

Common Automation Scenarios

Some of the most frequently automated workflows in enterprise environments include:

- **Invoice Processing and Approval**

- **Employee Onboarding and Offboarding**

- **Automated IT Ticket Triage**

- **Customer Service Escalations**

- **Data Synchronization Between Systems**

- **Scheduled Reports and Compliance Checks**

These tasks typically involve multiple systems, require orchestration logic, and benefit from event-driven, scalable architectures.

Architecture Pattern: Serverless Event-Driven Automation

A standard pattern for enterprise automation includes the following components:

1. **Trigger Source** – An event initiates the process (e.g., file upload, new email, database update).

2. **Logic App** – Acts as the orchestrator for steps such as parsing, validation, routing, and approvals.

3. **Azure Functions** – Perform custom logic like data transformation or calling external APIs.

4. **Storage** – Blob Storage, SQL Database, or Cosmos DB store intermediate or final data.

5. **Messaging Layer** – Azure Service Bus or Event Grid for reliable event handling.

Use Case: Invoice Processing System

Let's walk through a real-world invoice processing workflow automated using Azure serverless tools.

Step 1: Receiving and Storing the Invoice

Invoices arrive via email. A Logic App with the Office 365 connector listens for new attachments in a specific inbox and saves them to Blob Storage.

Logic App Trigger

- Trigger: When a new email arrives with attachment

- Action: Save attachment to Azure Blob Storage

- Action: Send event to Event Grid

Step 2: Event Grid Triggers Azure Function

Event Grid notifies an Azure Function that a new invoice has been uploaded.

```
public static class InvoiceParser
{
    [FunctionName("InvoiceParser")]
    public static async Task Run(
        [EventGridTrigger] EventGridEvent eventGridEvent,
        ILogger log)
    {
        var blobUrl = eventGridEvent.Data.ToString(); // parse Blob
URL

        // Download, extract data, and validate
        log.LogInformation($"Processing invoice from: {blobUrl}");
    }
}
```

The function extracts invoice metadata (vendor, amount, date) and stores it in a SQL Database.

Step 3: Approval Workflow

A Logic App initiates an approval request to a manager via Teams or email. The Logic App waits for a response using a **Wait for Response** action.

- If approved: Trigger payment processing

- If rejected: Send notification and log issue

Step 4: Integration with Finance System

An Azure Function handles API calls to the ERP or finance system (e.g., SAP, Dynamics 365).

```javascript
const axios = require("axios");

module.exports = async function (context, req) {
    const invoiceData = req.body;

    const response = await axios.post("https://api.finance-system.com/pay", invoiceData);

    context.res = {
        status: response.status,
        body: response.data
    };
};
```

Step 5: Audit Logging and Notification

All actions are logged in an Azure Table Storage for audit purposes. A final Logic App step sends confirmation to the vendor.

Security and Compliance Considerations

Enterprise workflows must follow strict compliance and security requirements. Serverless tools support these through:

- **Managed Identities** – Securely authenticate between Logic Apps, Functions, and resources without credentials.

- **Key Vault Integration** – Store API keys, connection strings, and secrets securely.

- **Private Endpoints and VNETs** – Isolate Logic Apps and Functions from public internet.

- **Role-Based Access Control (RBAC)** – Limit access to workflows and execution rights.

- **Audit Logs and Diagnostic Settings** – Enable monitoring for every action for regulatory compliance.

```
{
  "type": "Microsoft.Insights/diagnosticSettings",
  "properties": {
    "workspaceId": "[parameters('logAnalyticsWorkspaceId')]",
    "logs": [
      {
        "category": "WorkflowRuntime",
        "enabled": true
      }
    ]
  }
}
```

Monitoring and Maintenance

Using Azure Monitor and Application Insights, enterprises can ensure reliable and observable automation pipelines.

- Enable distributed tracing between Logic Apps and Azure Functions.

- Use alerts for failed Logic App runs or high failure rates in functions.

- Dashboard KPIs like invoices processed, average approval time, and error rates.

KQL Example: Failed Invoice Processing

```
requests
| where operation_Name == "InvoiceParser"
| where success == false
| summarize count() by resultCode, bin(timestamp, 1h)
```

Scaling for High-Volume Processing

In large enterprises, invoice volume may reach thousands per hour. Scaling can be addressed through:

- **Event Grid**: High-throughput ingestion

- **Function App Premium Plan**: No cold starts and support for VNET

- **Batching and Parallel Processing**: Process 100 invoices concurrently using queue-triggered Functions

Queue Trigger Example

```
public static async Task Run(
    [QueueTrigger("invoice-queue", Connection =
"AzureWebJobsStorage")] string message,
    ILogger log)
{
    var invoice = JsonConvert.DeserializeObject<Invoice>(message);
    // Process invoice
}
```

This model allows horizontal scaling with multiple function instances pulling from the queue simultaneously.

Additional Use Cases in Enterprises

HR Automation

- Onboarding Logic App triggered by new employee record

- Creates email account, schedules orientation, and generates badges

- Notifies IT and manager via Teams

IT Operations

- Auto-triage Logic App for incoming service desk tickets

- Tags high-priority tickets and routes them to the correct support group

- Azure Function checks CMDB to validate impacted systems

Legal and Compliance

- Document review workflow using Form Recognizer

- Logic App routes extracted text to legal reviewers

- Azure Function flags sensitive data for redaction

Best Practices

- **Break workflows into modular units** (microservices pattern)

- **Use retries and exception handling** in Logic Apps and Functions

- **Apply rate limits** and implement backoff strategies with queues

- **Tag resources** for cost attribution (e.g., Department=Finance)

- **Encrypt sensitive data at rest and in transit**

- **Version workflows** to manage changes safely

Summary

Enterprise automation is one of the strongest use cases for serverless technology on Azure. With the right combination of Logic Apps for orchestration and Azure Functions for custom logic, organizations can eliminate manual bottlenecks, enforce consistent processes, and respond dynamically to events—all while reducing operational costs and complexity.

The serverless model allows these workflows to scale as needed, be updated independently, and integrate deeply with both Microsoft and third-party services. By using enterprise-grade governance, security, and observability features, teams can confidently deploy serverless automation in even the most regulated industries.

In the next section, we'll explore how similar patterns are applied to ingest and process real-time IoT data using Azure's event-driven services.

IoT Data Ingestion and Processing

The proliferation of Internet of Things (IoT) devices in manufacturing, logistics, healthcare, agriculture, and smart city infrastructure has led to a surge in the need for scalable, reliable, and cost-effective data ingestion and processing pipelines. Serverless technologies on Azure are uniquely suited to address these challenges by providing event-driven architectures, automatic scaling, and integration with time-series databases, analytics engines, and AI services.

This section explores how Azure Functions, Event Hub, IoT Hub, Stream Analytics, and other serverless services can be orchestrated to ingest, process, analyze, and respond to high-volume IoT data streams in near real-time.

IoT Architecture Overview

A typical serverless IoT data pipeline on Azure includes:

1. **Azure IoT Hub** – Device-to-cloud communication channel for telemetry ingestion.

2. **Azure Event Hub** – High-throughput message ingestion and buffering.

3. **Azure Functions** – Event-driven compute to transform and route data.

4. **Azure Stream Analytics** – Real-time analytics and query engine.

5. **Azure Data Lake / Cosmos DB** – Long-term storage and querying.

6. **Power BI / Azure Monitor** – Visualization and alerting.

Ingesting Data with Azure IoT Hub

Azure IoT Hub is a fully managed service that acts as a central message hub for bi-directional communication between IoT applications and the devices they manage. It supports millions of simultaneous device connections and integrates natively with Event Hub-compatible endpoints.

Setting Up an IoT Hub

You can deploy an IoT Hub using Azure CLI:

```
az iot hub create \
  --name MyIoTHub \
  --resource-group MyResourceGroup \
  --sku S1
```

Once created, you can register devices:

```
az iot hub device-identity create \
  --hub-name MyIoTHub \
  --device-id sensor001
```

Devices can then send telemetry using MQTT, AMQP, or HTTPS protocols.

Sample Device-to-Cloud Telemetry (Python)

```python
from azure.iot.device import IoTHubDeviceClient, Message
import random

device_connection_string = "<your-device-connection-string>"
client =
IoTHubDeviceClient.create_from_connection_string(device_connection_s
tring)

temperature = 20 + random.random() * 15
humidity = 60 + random.random() * 20

msg = Message(f'{{"temperature": {temperature}, "humidity":
{humidity}}}')
client.send_message(msg)
```

This sends JSON-formatted telemetry every few seconds to the IoT Hub.

Stream Routing with Azure Event Hub

While IoT Hub supports routing directly to Azure Services, for broader scalability, many solutions send data to Event Hub, which is optimized for ingesting millions of events per second.

IoT Hub can forward messages to an Event Hub-compatible endpoint, which Azure Functions can then subscribe to.

Azure Function Triggered by Event Hub

```csharp
public static class TelemetryProcessor
{
    [FunctionName("TelemetryProcessor")]
    public static void Run(
        [EventHubTrigger("telemetry-hub", Connection =
"EventHubConnection")] string[] events,
        ILogger log)
    {
        foreach (var eventData in events)
        {
            log.LogInformation($"Received telemetry: {eventData}");
            // Parse, transform, or route data
        }
    }
}
```

Transforming and Storing IoT Data

You can enrich telemetry data using metadata (e.g., device location, type), convert it to a common format, and store it in databases for querying or further processing.

Writing to Azure Table Storage (C#)

```
CloudStorageAccount storageAccount =
CloudStorageAccount.Parse(connectionString);
CloudTableClient tableClient =
storageAccount.CreateCloudTableClient();
CloudTable table = tableClient.GetTableReference("TelemetryData");

var entity = new DynamicTableEntity("sensor001",
Guid.NewGuid().ToString());
entity.Properties.Add("Temperature", new EntityProperty(22.5));
entity.Properties.Add("Humidity", new EntityProperty(65));
await table.ExecuteAsync(TableOperation.Insert(entity));
```

This allows fast, scalable inserts with minimal cost.

Real-Time Processing with Stream Analytics

Azure Stream Analytics provides a powerful SQL-like language for analyzing telemetry streams in real time. It integrates directly with Event Hub, IoT Hub, and Azure Functions.

Example: High Temperature Alert

```
SELECT
    deviceId,
    AVG(temperature) AS avg_temp
INTO
    outputFunction
FROM
    telemetryStream TIMESTAMP BY eventEnqueuedUtcTime
GROUP BY
    TumblingWindow(minute, 1),
    deviceId
HAVING
    avg_temp > 40
```

This query calculates the average temperature every minute and forwards results to an Azure Function or Logic App if a threshold is exceeded.

Visualization with Power BI

Stream Analytics can also push data to Power BI datasets in real time for dashboards and live monitoring.

```
SELECT
    deviceId,
    temperature,
    humidity,
    eventEnqueuedUtcTime
INTO
    [PowerBIOutput]
FROM
    telemetryStream
```

This enables real-time dashboards for operations teams to monitor system health, alerts, and trends.

Machine Learning and Predictive Maintenance

Azure IoT data streams can be enriched with AI models to detect anomalies or predict failures. Models can be trained in Azure Machine Learning or with external libraries and deployed in Azure Functions or containers.

Predictive Maintenance Workflow

1. Data ingested from sensors via IoT Hub

2. Streamed to Azure Function

3. ML model evaluates condition (e.g., vibration, temperature)

4. If anomaly detected:

   o Log event

   o Notify engineer via Logic App

   o Trigger preventive action

Python Example with Scikit-learn Model

```
import joblib
import numpy as np

model = joblib.load("model.pkl")
```

```
def predict(data):
    values = np.array([[data["temp"], data["vibration"],
data["pressure"]]])
    prediction = model.predict(values)
    return prediction[0]
```

This logic can be wrapped in an HTTP-triggered Azure Function.

Security and Governance

IoT solutions must be built with strong security from device to cloud:

- **Per-device authentication** with unique keys or certificates

- **TLS encryption** for all data in transit

- **Azure Defender for IoT** for anomaly detection and threat modeling

- **Role-based access control (RBAC)** to restrict administrative access

- **Azure Policy** to enforce configurations like minimum TLS version or required tags

IoT Hub Access Policy (Read-only)

```
az iot hub policy create \
  --hub-name MyIoTHub \
  --name ReaderPolicy \
  --permissions RegistryRead ServiceConnect
```

This ensures least-privilege access for read-only consumers of telemetry data.

Scaling Considerations

IoT systems must scale to support:

- Thousands or millions of connected devices

- High-frequency telemetry (e.g., 1 message/second/device)

- Multi-region redundancy

Azure supports scale via:

- **IoT Hub units** (each unit supports ~4000 messages/sec)

- **Event Hub partitions**

- **Function App Premium Plans** with high-concurrency execution

- **Geo-distributed storage and Cosmos DB**

Partitioning and batching are essential. Use device IDs to shard data into Event Hub partitions or Cosmos DB logical partitions.

Error Handling and Resilience

IoT data is susceptible to network interruptions, malformed messages, or device faults. Best practices include:

- **Dead-letter queues** for unprocessable messages

- **Retry logic** in Functions and downstream systems

- **Device twins** to store last known status or sync commands

- **Batch processing** to reduce IOPS and cost

Handling Malformed Payloads in Azure Function

```
try
{
    var data = JsonConvert.DeserializeObject<Telemetry>(input);
    // process
}
catch (JsonException ex)
{
    log.LogError($"Failed to parse telemetry: {ex.Message}");
    // Optionally route to dead-letter storage
}
```

Governance and Cost Management

Monitoring usage and cost is critical in IoT scenarios. Use:

- Azure Cost Management to track Event Hub and Function consumption

- Resource tags for grouping by product or department

- Budgets and alerts on Function App executions or telemetry volume

- Azure Monitor for per-device metrics, failure rates, and latency

IoT Hub tiers and message quotas should be evaluated monthly. Avoid overprovisioning by starting with S1 or B1 and scaling as needed.

Summary

Azure's serverless ecosystem provides the backbone for robust, scalable, and intelligent IoT data pipelines. By combining Azure IoT Hub, Event Hub, Azure Functions, and Stream Analytics, enterprises can process massive volumes of device telemetry in real time, react intelligently to anomalies, and unlock insights that drive business value.

Whether used for predictive maintenance, supply chain optimization, or smart energy management, the serverless model minimizes operational overhead and enables rapid innovation in the IoT domain. Next, we'll see how these same technologies can be applied to enhance customer experiences in e-commerce platforms.

E-commerce and Customer Engagement Systems

In the dynamic and competitive landscape of digital commerce, delivering fast, personalized, and reliable user experiences is critical to business success. Serverless technologies on Azure enable e-commerce platforms to handle unpredictable traffic, perform real-time personalization, process transactions efficiently, and drive customer engagement without the burden of managing infrastructure.

This section explores how Azure Functions, Logic Apps, Event Grid, and serverless integrations with databases and messaging systems can be used to build responsive and intelligent e-commerce applications. We'll also examine patterns for scaling, personalization, analytics, and customer interaction workflows.

Key Requirements in E-commerce

Modern e-commerce systems must address the following:

- **High Availability and Elastic Scalability** – Seamless experience during peak traffic (e.g., Black Friday).

- **Real-Time Personalization** – Tailored content and recommendations.

- **Order Processing and Inventory Updates** – Accurate and quick backend processing.

- **Event-Driven Notifications** – Email/SMS/Push alerts for order confirmations, shipping, and promotions.

- **Customer Support Automation** – AI bots, ticket routing, feedback loops.

- **Analytics and Insights** – Conversion rates, customer journeys, A/B testing.

Serverless tools in Azure provide the capabilities to meet these goals efficiently.

Event-Driven Architecture for E-commerce

A sample serverless e-commerce platform may use:

- **Frontend**: Static site on Azure Static Web Apps or frontend hosted on App Service.

- **Backend APIs**: Azure Functions for catalog lookup, cart actions, checkout, and more.

- **Event Grid**: Routes events like "order placed", "payment failed", "item shipped".

- **Logic Apps**: Orchestrate backend workflows such as sending emails or updating CRM.

- **Cosmos DB / SQL Database**: Store products, users, orders.

- **Azure Notification Hubs**: Push mobile and browser notifications.

- **Azure Cognitive Services**: Chatbots, recommendation engines, sentiment analysis.

Customer Interaction Workflow: Cart and Checkout

Azure Functions for Cart Management

Functions handle real-time cart logic.

```
module.exports = async function (context, req) {
    const { userId, itemId, quantity } = req.body;
    // Fetch current cart from Cosmos DB
    // Update quantity or add new item
    // Save and return updated cart
    context.res = {
        status: 200,
        body: { message: "Cart updated successfully" }
    };
};
```

Functions scale independently per user, handling spikes in add-to-cart actions without server strain.

Checkout Logic with Orchestration

A Durable Function can manage a multi-step checkout process:

1. Validate payment

2. Reserve inventory

3. Generate invoice

4. Send confirmation email

5. Update CRM

```
[FunctionName("CheckoutOrchestration")]
public static async Task RunOrchestrator(
    [OrchestrationTrigger] IDurableOrchestrationContext context)
{
    var order = context.GetInput<Order>();
    await context.CallActivityAsync("ValidatePayment", order);
    await context.CallActivityAsync("ReserveInventory", order);
    await context.CallActivityAsync("SendInvoice", order);
    await context.CallActivityAsync("NotifyCustomer", order);
}
```

Durable Functions provide resilience and state management, allowing retries and status tracking for each step.

Order Processing and Inventory Management

Once a user completes a purchase, an event is emitted. Azure Event Grid routes this event to multiple subscribers:

- An Azure Function updates inventory.

- A Logic App sends an order confirmation.

- A Service Bus Queue forwards the message to the warehouse system.

Event Grid Subscription Example
```
az eventgrid event-subscription create \
```

```
--name order-processor \
--source-resource-id /subscriptions/.../topics/order-events \
--endpoint https://<function-url>
```

This allows fan-out of a single event to multiple systems.

Inventory Update Function (C#)

```csharp
public static class UpdateInventory
{
    [FunctionName("UpdateInventory")]
    public static async Task Run(
        [EventGridTrigger] EventGridEvent eventGridEvent,
        ILogger log)
    {
        var order =
JsonConvert.DeserializeObject<Order>(eventGridEvent.Data.ToString())
;
        foreach (var item in order.Items)
        {
            // Deduct item.Quantity from stock in Cosmos DB
        }
        log.LogInformation("Inventory updated.");
    }
}
```

Inventory accuracy is ensured with atomic writes and optimistic concurrency in Cosmos DB.

Personalized Recommendations

Azure Functions can serve personalized product recommendations using a pre-trained model or Azure Personalizer.

Workflow

1. On page load or user login, Function is triggered.

2. User profile data is fetched.

3. Function queries recommendation model or API.

4. Top items are returned to the frontend.

Example: Using Azure Personalizer

```javascript
const axios = require("axios");

module.exports = async function (context, req) {
    const userFeatures = req.body.userFeatures;

    const response = await axios.post(
        "https://<your-personalizer-endpoint>/rank",
        {
            contextFeatures: userFeatures,
            actions: productList
        },
        { headers: { "Ocp-Apim-Subscription-Key": "<your-key>" } }
    );

    context.res = {
        body: response.data.rewardActionId
    };
};
```

This real-time ranking service can significantly increase conversions.

Customer Notifications and Engagement

Logic App: Order Confirmation via Email

- Trigger: Event Grid event "orderConfirmed"

- Actions:

    - Look up customer email in database

    - Format email content using HTML template

    - Send via SendGrid or Office 365 connector

Push Notifications with Azure Notification Hubs

- Mobile app subscribes to user-specific tags.

- Azure Function pushes update:

```csharp
var hub =
NotificationHubClient.CreateClientFromConnectionString(...);
```

```
await hub.SendGcmNativeNotificationAsync("{ \"data\" :
{\"message\":\"Your order has shipped!\"}}", "user_1234");
```

Targeted push notifications drive re-engagement and inform users of key milestones.

A/B Testing and Feature Flags

Azure App Configuration and Azure Front Door allow real-time feature management.

- Define flags like showNewCart, enableQuickCheckout.

- Use Azure Functions to check flags per request:

```
var config = new ConfigurationClient("<app-config-connection-
string>");
var feature = await
config.GetConfigurationSettingAsync("feature:enableQuickCheckout");
```

Split traffic based on flag value, user segments, or geo-location, allowing experimentation and gradual rollouts.

Analytics and Conversion Tracking

Azure Monitor and Application Insights can track:

- Conversion rates

- Funnel drop-off points

- Product page views

- Average time to checkout

- Failed payments

Sample KQL: Cart Abandonment Rate

```
customEvents
| where name == "CartUpdated"
| summarize count() by user_Id
| join kind=leftanti (
    customEvents | where name == "CheckoutComplete"
    | summarize count() by user_Id
) on user_Id
```

This identifies users who added to cart but didn't complete checkout, useful for remarketing or UX improvements.

Scaling Considerations

E-commerce traffic can spike rapidly. Azure's serverless model supports elastic scaling through:

- **Function App Premium Plan**: Handles high-concurrency, no cold starts.

- **Event Grid + Service Bus**: Decouples processing from user flow.

- **Cosmos DB with partitioning**: Ensures high-throughput reads/writes.

- **Front Door / CDN**: Global caching for performance and cost optimization.

Peak readiness checklist:

- Warm up key Azure Functions

- Pre-scale Cosmos DB throughput

- Enable autoscale rules for Logic Apps

- Queue non-critical tasks (e.g., CRM updates) for async handling

Fraud Detection and Security

Use Azure tools to monitor and prevent fraudulent activities:

- **Azure Sentinel**: SIEM for real-time threat detection.

- **IP restrictions and WAF**: Protect APIs and endpoints.

- **Rate limiting** via Azure API Management

- **Bot Protection** using Cognitive Services

- **Logging** and correlation IDs for forensic tracing

Summary

Building serverless e-commerce solutions on Azure allows developers to focus on creating seamless, personalized, and responsive shopping experiences while Azure handles scale, security, and reliability. By leveraging Azure Functions, Logic Apps, and Event Grid, businesses can automate order processing, personalize content, and maintain customer engagement with minimal infrastructure overhead.

This architecture supports rapid innovation and adapts to changing business needs, making it ideal for modern commerce. In the next chapter, we will examine how emerging trends like AI, edge computing, and serverless containers are shaping the future of serverless computing on Azure.

Chapter 10: Future of Serverless on Azure

Trends and Innovations in Serverless Architecture

The future of serverless computing on Azure is shaped by a combination of emerging technologies, evolving customer needs, and improvements in the underlying infrastructure. Serverless computing, which abstracts the management of servers, has become an essential part of the cloud ecosystem due to its simplicity, scalability, and cost efficiency. As businesses increasingly adopt serverless architectures, Azure continues to innovate and expand its offerings to stay ahead in this dynamic landscape. This section explores the current trends and future innovations that will shape the evolution of serverless on Azure.

1. Serverless and Microservices

One of the significant trends in the serverless landscape is the integration of serverless computing with microservices architectures. Microservices are a pattern where applications are broken down into smaller, independent services, each responsible for a specific business function. These services are loosely coupled and can scale independently.

Serverless computing complements microservices perfectly by enabling automatic scaling, reduced operational overhead, and efficient resource usage. Azure Functions, as part of Azure's serverless suite, is designed to support microservices-based architectures. Developers can design each function as an independent unit of work that performs a specific task. Functions can be triggered by different events such as HTTP requests, message queues, or changes in databases, allowing them to operate in an event-driven manner.

Azure Kubernetes Service (AKS) also plays a key role in this trend by enabling Kubernetes-based containerized microservices to be seamlessly integrated with serverless functions. Through Azure Functions for Kubernetes, you can deploy and manage functions within a Kubernetes cluster, blending the best of both worlds: serverless and containerized microservices.

As the microservices approach continues to gain popularity, serverless computing will likely become more integrated with containerized environments, supporting both lightweight, event-driven execution and the flexibility of Kubernetes for orchestration.

2. AI and Serverless: A Perfect Combination

Artificial intelligence (AI) is another area where serverless computing is making significant strides. By combining serverless computing with AI and machine learning, Azure enables developers to build sophisticated, scalable, and cost-effective AI-powered applications.

Azure's serverless offerings, such as Azure Functions and Logic Apps, are increasingly being used in conjunction with AI services like Azure Cognitive Services, Azure Machine Learning, and Azure Bot Services. These services allow developers to integrate pre-built AI models for tasks like natural language processing, computer vision, and predictive analytics without having to manage the underlying infrastructure.

For example, you can use Azure Functions to trigger AI-based workflows, such as processing images for object detection or running sentiment analysis on incoming customer feedback. Azure Logic Apps can integrate AI models into more complex business workflows, automating tasks like generating insights from unstructured data or providing real-time recommendations.

The growing demand for AI capabilities in cloud applications will drive innovations in serverless computing, allowing AI workloads to scale automatically based on demand without worrying about resource provisioning or management.

3. Event-Driven Architectures and Streamlining Operations

Event-driven architectures (EDAs) are gaining popularity in modern cloud-native applications. EDAs focus on building systems that respond to events or changes in the system, such as user actions, sensor data, or external API calls. Azure is at the forefront of supporting event-driven architectures with services like Azure Event Grid, Azure Service Bus, and Azure Event Hubs, all of which integrate seamlessly with Azure Functions and Logic Apps.

Azure Event Grid, for instance, simplifies the creation of event-driven applications by enabling the routing of events from different sources to the appropriate functions or services. This model allows developers to build decoupled, scalable systems that react to real-time events without needing to worry about managing infrastructure. Event-driven architectures are particularly useful for scenarios like notifications, real-time analytics, and microservices communication.

In the future, Azure will continue to evolve its event-driven capabilities, enabling even greater scalability, reliability, and flexibility. We can expect more robust integration between event-driven systems and other Azure services, making it easier for developers to build complex workflows that are triggered by events, such as processing streams of data or responding to user interactions in real-time.

4. Serverless for Hybrid and Multi-Cloud Environments

As organizations adopt hybrid and multi-cloud strategies, there is a growing need for serverless solutions that can seamlessly operate across different cloud environments. Azure has made significant strides in enabling hybrid cloud scenarios with services like Azure Arc, which extends Azure's management capabilities to on-premises, multi-cloud, and edge environments.

Azure Arc enables serverless applications to run on any infrastructure, allowing businesses to deploy serverless functions across different clouds, including AWS and Google Cloud, while maintaining centralized control and management. This is particularly valuable for organizations that need to meet specific compliance, data sovereignty, or latency requirements that might necessitate running workloads in multiple clouds.

In addition to Azure Arc, there are also innovations in how serverless computing can be optimized for edge computing scenarios. Azure IoT Edge allows you to deploy serverless functions to edge devices, enabling real-time data processing at the source. This capability is crucial for scenarios like autonomous vehicles, industrial automation, and smart cities, where low-latency processing and localized decision-making are critical.

The future of serverless in hybrid and multi-cloud environments will see further improvements in interoperability, security, and governance, making it easier for organizations to leverage the full power of serverless computing, regardless of where their workloads are hosted.

5. Improved Developer Experiences with Serverless

One of the key areas of focus for Azure is improving the developer experience when building serverless applications. As serverless computing becomes more popular, Azure is continually enhancing its tools and services to make it easier for developers to build, test, and deploy serverless applications.

Azure Functions 4.x introduces features like dependency injection and improved local debugging, making it easier for developers to build and test serverless functions in their local environments. The Azure Functions Core Tools and the Azure Functions extension for Visual Studio Code provide a seamless development experience, allowing developers to test and deploy their functions with minimal friction.

In addition, Azure Logic Apps offers a no-code/low-code environment that allows non-developers to build automated workflows using a visual designer. This democratization of automation empowers business users to create serverless workflows without needing deep technical knowledge, opening up new opportunities for citizen developers.

Azure will continue to improve these tools and integrate them with other development platforms, making it easier for developers to adopt serverless architectures and build applications faster and more efficiently.

6. The Future of Serverless Databases

Serverless databases, like Azure Cosmos DB, are also evolving to meet the demands of modern cloud applications. Azure Cosmos DB already offers a serverless tier that automatically scales to handle variable workloads, making it ideal for scenarios where traffic is unpredictable or variable.

As the need for real-time, globally distributed databases grows, serverless databases will become even more critical in serverless architectures. Future innovations will likely focus on improving performance, reducing latency, and enhancing the ability to handle large-scale data processing with minimal cost.

In addition, we can expect to see more serverless database options for specialized use cases, such as time-series data, graph databases, and document storage, all of which can be integrated seamlessly with serverless compute resources like Azure Functions and Logic Apps.

Conclusion

The future of serverless computing on Azure is filled with exciting possibilities. As organizations continue to embrace cloud-native architectures, Azure's serverless offerings will evolve to support new patterns, tools, and services that simplify application development and enhance scalability, performance, and cost efficiency. The integration of serverless with microservices, AI, event-driven architectures, hybrid cloud environments, and edge computing will drive innovation and create new opportunities for businesses to build modern, efficient, and intelligent applications.

By continuing to innovate and improve the developer experience, Azure will remain at the forefront of the serverless revolution, empowering developers to focus on building the next generation of cloud-native applications without worrying about infrastructure management. The future is bright for serverless on Azure, and it will undoubtedly play a central role in shaping the future of cloud computing.

Expanding with AI and Machine Learning

The integration of Artificial Intelligence (AI) and Machine Learning (ML) into serverless computing is rapidly transforming the landscape of cloud-based applications. Serverless computing allows organizations to scale their AI and ML workloads without worrying about the underlying infrastructure. This section delves into how AI and ML can be expanded within a serverless framework, particularly focusing on how Azure's serverless services can be used to build sophisticated, scalable, and cost-efficient AI-powered applications.

The Growing Role of AI and Machine Learning

AI and ML are becoming essential components of modern applications. From image recognition and natural language processing (NLP) to recommendation systems and predictive analytics, AI and ML enable businesses to create intelligent applications that can learn, adapt, and improve over time. As cloud computing continues to evolve, serverless computing provides an ideal platform for running these workloads because it automatically handles resource allocation, scaling, and high availability.

Azure provides several tools and services that make it easier to integrate AI and ML into serverless applications. These include Azure Cognitive Services, Azure Machine Learning, and Azure Databricks. By combining these tools with serverless compute services like Azure Functions and Azure Logic Apps, developers can build robust AI-powered solutions without the need for complex infrastructure management.

Leveraging Azure Cognitive Services

Azure Cognitive Services provides a suite of pre-built AI models that developers can integrate into their applications with minimal effort. These services cover a wide range of use cases, including computer vision, speech recognition, language understanding, and decision-making. By incorporating these cognitive capabilities into serverless functions, developers can build intelligent applications that process images, videos, text, and speech on the fly, all without having to train their own AI models.

For example, Azure's Computer Vision API can analyze images and extract valuable insights such as object detection, text recognition, and facial analysis. This can be integrated with Azure Functions to trigger AI-powered workflows whenever a new image is uploaded to a storage account. The following code snippet shows how to use Azure Functions to process images using the Computer Vision API:

```javascript
const axios = require('axios');
const { DefaultAzureCredential } = require('@azure/identity');

module.exports = async function (context, req) {
    const imageUrl = req.query.imageUrl;
    const credential = new DefaultAzureCredential();
    const endpoint = "<YOUR_COGNITIVE_SERVICE_ENDPOINT>";
    const key = "<YOUR_COGNITIVE_SERVICE_KEY>";

    const headers = {
        'Ocp-Apim-Subscription-Key': key,
        'Content-Type': 'application/json'
    };

    const body = {
        url: imageUrl
    };

    try {
        const response = await
axios.post(`${endpoint}/vision/v3.2/analyze?visualFeatures=Descripti
on`, body, { headers });
        context.res = {
            status: 200,
            body: response.data
        };
    } catch (error) {
        context.res = {
            status: 500,
            body: error.message
        };
    }
};
```

In this example, whenever an image URL is passed to the function, it triggers the Cognitive Services API to analyze the image and return the results, such as a description of the objects detected. This functionality can be integrated into workflows to automatically trigger actions, such as sending a notification if specific objects are detected, or saving the analysis results to a database.

Building Custom AI Models with Azure Machine Learning

While Azure Cognitive Services provides powerful pre-built models, there are times when businesses need to build and train their own AI models to meet specific requirements. Azure Machine Learning (Azure ML) is a comprehensive cloud-based environment that allows data scientists and developers to build, train, and deploy machine learning models at scale.

Azure ML provides a serverless compute option called Azure ML Pipelines, which allows developers to create end-to-end machine learning workflows that can be executed in a serverless manner. By combining Azure Functions with Azure ML, developers can trigger machine learning tasks based on events or user interactions, enabling real-time AI predictions and decision-making.

For example, suppose you are building a recommendation system for an e-commerce platform. You can use Azure ML to train a model on user behavior data and deploy it as a web service. The following code snippet shows how to invoke an Azure ML web service using Azure Functions:

```python
import requests
import json

def main(req):
    model_endpoint = "<YOUR_MODEL_ENDPOINT>"
    headers = {
        'Content-Type': 'application/json',
        'Authorization': 'Bearer <YOUR_API_KEY>'
    }

    data = {
        "input_data": req.get_json()
    }

    response = requests.post(model_endpoint, headers=headers, json=data)

    if response.status_code == 200:
        return response.json()
    else:
        return {
```

```
        "status": "error",
        "message": response.text
    }
```

In this example, the Azure Function triggers the machine learning model hosted on Azure ML and sends input data in JSON format. The model returns a prediction or recommendation, which can then be used to trigger further actions, such as suggesting products to the user or personalizing the experience in real time.

Real-Time AI Workflows with Logic Apps

While Azure Functions is well-suited for event-driven serverless computing, Azure Logic Apps provides a powerful low-code/drag-and-drop solution for automating complex workflows, including those that involve AI and ML. Logic Apps can integrate with AI services and Azure Functions, enabling developers to build end-to-end, serverless workflows that respond to real-time events.

For instance, you can design a workflow that listens for new customer feedback submitted via a form. When the form is submitted, the feedback data can be passed through a sentiment analysis model using Azure Cognitive Services' Text Analytics API. If the sentiment is negative, the workflow can trigger an automatic alert or create a support ticket in a help desk system.

Here's an example of how such a workflow could be structured:

1. **Trigger**: New customer feedback is submitted via a web form (e.g., via an HTTP trigger).

2. **Action 1**: The feedback is sent to the Text Analytics API for sentiment analysis.

3. **Action 2**: Based on the sentiment analysis, an email is sent to the customer service team if the sentiment is negative.

4. **Action 3**: If the sentiment is positive, a thank-you message is sent to the customer.

This entire process can be automated using Azure Logic Apps, enabling a serverless, event-driven workflow for real-time AI-powered decision-making.

Serverless AI with Azure Databricks

Azure Databricks is a fast, easy, and collaborative Apache Spark-based analytics platform that accelerates data engineering and data science workloads. It is particularly useful for big data processing, advanced analytics, and machine learning. Databricks provides a fully managed environment that allows you to process large datasets in parallel and scale your workloads automatically.

By integrating Azure Databricks with Azure Functions, you can create a serverless architecture that processes massive amounts of data in real-time. For example, a streaming data pipeline might ingest log data, process it using Spark, and apply ML models in real-time to generate insights. Azure Functions can then trigger actions based on these insights, such as storing results in a database, sending alerts, or invoking other services.

Future of AI and Serverless

Looking ahead, AI and machine learning are expected to be more deeply integrated with serverless platforms like Azure, enabling even more powerful and scalable applications. As machine learning models become more complex and computationally intensive, serverless computing will provide the elasticity needed to handle these workloads. Innovations such as serverless AI model training and deployment, automatic scaling of AI services, and improved integration with edge computing will open up new possibilities for AI-powered applications.

Azure's continued investment in AI and ML will make it easier for developers to build intelligent, data-driven applications without worrying about infrastructure management. The combination of serverless computing with AI and ML offers an ideal solution for businesses looking to innovate and scale their applications quickly while keeping costs low and operational complexity at a minimum.

The future of serverless and AI is intertwined, and as both fields evolve, we will see even more seamless integration, allowing businesses to leverage the full power of AI and machine learning in a cost-effective and scalable manner. Azure will continue to be at the forefront of this transformation, offering developers the tools and capabilities to build the next generation of intelligent, serverless applications.

Recommendations for Staying Ahead

In the rapidly evolving world of serverless computing on Azure, it's essential for developers, architects, and businesses to stay ahead of the curve to leverage the full potential of serverless architecture. The future of serverless is shaped by ongoing innovations and the growing adoption of new technologies, and staying ahead requires proactive learning, adaptation, and integration of these advancements. This section outlines key recommendations for staying ahead in the serverless domain on Azure.

1. Embrace a Serverless Mindset

The first step to staying ahead is adopting a serverless mindset. This mindset is characterized by focusing on the application's business logic and letting the cloud provider, in this case, Azure, manage the underlying infrastructure. Serverless computing abstracts away the complexities of managing virtual machines, networks, and databases. Instead of worrying about scaling, patching, or provisioning servers, developers can focus on writing code that performs specific tasks.

Azure Functions, Logic Apps, and other serverless offerings make it easier to follow this approach. When building applications, consider how each component can be decoupled and broken into smaller, independent services that respond to specific events. This allows for faster iteration, lower costs, and better scalability as applications grow.

To stay ahead, it's important to understand how to break down monolithic systems into smaller, event-driven components. This will not only improve application performance but also allow you to take full advantage of the scalability and cost-efficiency of serverless architectures.

2. Understand and Leverage Azure's Evolving Serverless Services

Azure is continuously evolving its serverless offerings to meet the needs of modern developers. Keeping up with the latest updates and new services is crucial. Azure Functions, for example, has seen several new features and performance improvements in recent years, such as enhanced debugging tools, integration with Azure DevOps and GitHub Actions, and expanded support for various programming languages.

Some of the critical advancements to look out for in the serverless space include:

- **Enhanced language support**: Azure Functions supports a wide range of programming languages, including JavaScript, Python, C#, Java, and PowerShell. As Azure introduces support for new languages, developers should be ready to explore and take advantage of these options.

- **Improved scaling capabilities**: One of the primary benefits of serverless computing is automatic scaling. Azure has made significant strides in improving the scaling mechanisms in serverless environments, ensuring that workloads are handled efficiently even during traffic spikes.

- **New event sources**: Azure constantly expands the number of event sources that can trigger Azure Functions. These event sources include Azure Event Grid, Azure Service Bus, HTTP requests, and storage events. Staying current on new event sources will allow developers to design more flexible and scalable architectures.

By staying up to date with these advancements, developers can ensure they are using the most efficient tools available to build scalable, performant serverless applications.

3. Master Azure DevOps and CI/CD Pipelines for Serverless

A crucial aspect of staying ahead is mastering the deployment and lifecycle management of serverless applications. While serverless architectures simplify many aspects of application management, they still require well-established DevOps practices to ensure efficient development, testing, and deployment workflows.

Azure DevOps and GitHub Actions provide robust tools to manage the continuous integration and continuous deployment (CI/CD) of serverless applications. With these tools, developers can automate testing, deployment, and monitoring processes, reducing manual intervention and speeding up the release cycle.

For example, setting up CI/CD pipelines for Azure Functions allows you to automatically deploy updates whenever changes are made to your codebase. Here's a basic example of how a GitHub Actions pipeline might look to deploy an Azure Function:

```yaml
name: Azure Functions CI/CD

on:
  push:
    branches:
      - main

jobs:
  build:
    runs-on: ubuntu-latest
    steps:
    - uses: actions/checkout@v2
    - name: Set up Node.js
      uses: actions/setup-node@v2
      with:
        node-version: '14'
    - name: Install dependencies
      run: npm install
    - name: Deploy to Azure
      uses: azure/functions-action@v1
      with:
        app-name: 'YOUR_FUNCTION_APP_NAME'
        publish-profile: ${{
secrets.AZURE_FUNCTION_APP_PUBLISH_PROFILE }}
```

This YAML configuration triggers the deployment of an Azure Function whenever changes are pushed to the main branch. Setting up CI/CD pipelines in this way ensures that new features or bug fixes are automatically deployed, reducing the time spent on manual deployments and minimizing errors.

4. Implement Cost Management Strategies

While serverless computing offers significant cost savings due to its pay-as-you-go model, it is essential to manage and optimize costs effectively. Without careful monitoring, serverless applications can become expensive if resources are not properly managed or if there are inefficient function calls. Azure provides several tools to help manage costs effectively, such as Azure Cost Management + Billing and Azure Monitor.

Here are some strategies to control costs in a serverless architecture:

- **Optimize function execution times**: The cost of using Azure Functions is primarily determined by the execution time and memory used. By optimizing the function code to run more efficiently, you can reduce execution time and memory consumption, ultimately lowering costs.

- **Use proper scaling configurations**: Ensure that Azure Functions are properly configured to scale according to demand. For instance, using the Consumption Plan for Azure Functions allows functions to automatically scale in response to incoming events without requiring you to manage scaling manually. On the other hand, if you anticipate high traffic, consider using the Premium Plan or Dedicated Plan for better performance at predictable costs.

- **Monitor usage with Azure Monitor**: Azure Monitor provides insights into the usage of serverless resources. Regularly reviewing performance metrics will help you spot inefficiencies and take corrective action.

Staying ahead in the cost management space requires constant monitoring and adapting your serverless workloads to avoid unnecessary expenses. Implementing these strategies will ensure that serverless applications remain cost-effective as they scale.

5. Focus on Security Best Practices

As with any cloud platform, security remains a primary concern when developing serverless applications. Serverless architectures can introduce unique security challenges, including securing access to serverless functions, ensuring data privacy, and preventing unauthorized execution of functions.

Azure provides several tools to improve the security posture of serverless applications:

- **Managed identities**: Managed identities in Azure provide an identity for Azure services to authenticate to other Azure resources without needing to store credentials in your code. Azure Functions can use managed identities to securely access other resources, such as Azure Key Vault, databases, or storage accounts, without requiring hard-coded credentials.

- **Key Vault integration**: For sensitive data, such as API keys, connection strings, or certificates, Azure Key Vault provides a secure place to store and manage secrets. Integrating Azure Functions with Key Vault ensures that sensitive information is never stored in the codebase.

- **API Management for function security**: Azure API Management can be used to create secure and controlled access to your Azure Functions. By configuring authentication, rate limiting, and logging, you can ensure that only authorized users and services can invoke your serverless functions.

By understanding and implementing security best practices, developers can reduce the risk of security breaches and ensure that their serverless applications are secure and compliant with industry standards.

6. Learn About Serverless at the Edge

Serverless computing is increasingly being integrated into edge computing environments. Edge computing allows data processing and computation to occur closer to the end users or devices, minimizing latency and improving performance. Azure offers a suite of edge computing solutions, such as Azure IoT Edge, which extends serverless functions to edge devices.

By staying ahead in edge computing, developers can take advantage of the benefits of serverless at the edge, such as real-time decision-making, reduced latency, and offline processing. Learning how to deploy and manage serverless functions at the edge will give developers a competitive edge in industries like IoT, autonomous systems, and smart cities.

7. Keep Exploring New Use Cases for Serverless

Finally, staying ahead means constantly exploring new use cases for serverless computing. As the technology evolves, new patterns and opportunities emerge. Serverless applications are now used in a wide range of scenarios, from simple web apps to complex event-driven architectures. Experimenting with different serverless patterns and architectures will allow you to identify new ways to leverage serverless computing for your business needs.

Some potential areas to explore include:

- **Real-time analytics**: Use Azure Functions to process streaming data in real-time and trigger actions based on the data. For example, serverless functions can be used in fraud detection systems, where every transaction is analyzed and flagged if suspicious activity is detected.

- **Serverless containers**: Although serverless computing is primarily known for functions, there's a growing trend of running containerized applications in a serverless environment. Azure Container Instances (ACI) can run containers without the need to manage the infrastructure, providing a serverless approach to containerized applications.

By continuously experimenting and learning, developers can stay ahead by discovering new ways to solve problems and create innovative serverless applications.

Conclusion

Staying ahead in the serverless landscape on Azure requires a proactive approach to learning, adopting new technologies, and implementing best practices. By embracing a serverless mindset, mastering the tools and services provided by Azure, optimizing cost and performance, and staying informed about new trends and innovations, developers can ensure that they remain at the forefront of the serverless revolution. Whether building intelligent AI-powered applications, implementing secure workflows, or leveraging edge computing, serverless on Azure offers endless possibilities for creating modern, scalable, and efficient applications.

Chapter 11: Appendices

Glossary of Terms

Serverless computing is rapidly gaining traction as an efficient and cost-effective solution for many developers and organizations. However, due to its relatively recent rise in popularity, some of its core concepts may not be immediately clear to all readers. This glossary aims to define and explain the key terms used throughout the book, especially in the context of Azure's serverless offerings. Whether you are new to serverless or an experienced cloud developer, having a solid understanding of these terms will enable you to better navigate and leverage Azure's serverless technologies.

Azure Functions

Azure Functions is a serverless compute service provided by Microsoft Azure that allows you to run small pieces of code, known as "functions," without having to manage infrastructure. You can trigger these functions with events, such as HTTP requests, database changes, or messages from a queue. Azure Functions automatically scales based on demand and charges only for the execution time, not the underlying infrastructure.

Logic Apps

Logic Apps is an Azure service that allows you to automate workflows and integrate apps, data, and services without writing any code. It provides a visual designer for creating workflows that can connect to various services such as databases, storage, email, and APIs. Logic Apps is primarily used for building integrations between applications, automating business processes, and orchestrating data flows across systems.

Event Grid

Event Grid is a fully managed event routing service in Azure that enables event-driven architectures by providing reliable event delivery. It allows different services to react to events in real time and ensures that your system is decoupled and scalable. Event Grid can integrate with services like Azure Functions, Logic Apps, and Azure Storage to trigger workflows based on specific events.

Durable Functions

Durable Functions is an extension of Azure Functions that enables the development of long-running workflows. Unlike regular functions, which are short-lived and stateless, Durable Functions allows you to manage complex workflows with multiple steps, including retries, human interactions, and long-running processes that can last hours, days, or even longer. Durable Functions maintains the state of the workflow across function calls and can scale automatically.

API Management

API Management is an Azure service that helps organizations to create, publish, secure, and monitor APIs. It provides tools for defining, versioning, and enforcing policies for APIs, making it easier for developers to integrate services and ensure secure, reliable access to backend systems. Azure API Management also enables rate-limiting, authentication, and logging for APIs, ensuring that they are used effectively and efficiently.

Bicep

Bicep is a Domain-Specific Language (DSL) for defining Azure resources in a declarative way. It simplifies the process of writing infrastructure as code (IaC) for Azure by providing a more concise and readable syntax than the traditional JSON-based Azure Resource Manager (ARM) templates. Bicep helps developers deploy and manage resources on Azure with a clearer, less error-prone syntax while still leveraging the power of Azure's ARM template system.

Azure Monitor

Azure Monitor is a comprehensive monitoring service that provides a unified pipeline for collecting, analyzing, and acting on telemetry data from Azure and on-premises environments. It helps organizations ensure the performance, availability, and security of their applications and infrastructure. Azure Monitor collects data from various sources, including applications, virtual machines, and Azure resources, and provides tools for querying, visualizing, and alerting on that data.

Managed Identity

Managed Identity is a feature in Azure Active Directory (Azure AD) that provides an identity for Azure services to authenticate to other Azure resources. Managed identities eliminate the need for hardcoded credentials in code and make it easier to implement secure, automated access to Azure resources. This feature is essential for serverless applications, as it allows functions and Logic Apps to authenticate and access resources such as databases or storage accounts securely.

Key Vault

Azure Key Vault is a cloud service for securely storing and managing sensitive information such as secrets, encryption keys, and certificates. It allows applications to retrieve keys and secrets securely at runtime, eliminating the need to store them in code or configuration files. Key Vault integrates with Azure Managed Identity, making it easy to control access to sensitive data and ensuring that only authorized users or applications can access it.

CI/CD (Continuous Integration/Continuous Deployment)

CI/CD is a set of best practices in modern software development aimed at automating the process of building, testing, and deploying software. Continuous Integration (CI) involves automatically integrating changes into the codebase, while Continuous Deployment (CD) involves automatically deploying those changes to production once they pass automated tests. For serverless applications, CI/CD pipelines help streamline the deployment process and ensure code quality and reliability.

ARM Templates

Azure Resource Manager (ARM) templates are JSON files used to define and deploy Azure resources in a declarative manner. These templates describe the infrastructure and configuration needed for an Azure solution, and they can be reused and version-controlled for consistent deployments. ARM templates allow developers to define resources such as virtual machines, databases, and networking components, as well as configure them in a repeatable and reliable way.

Cold Start

Cold start is the initial latency experienced when invoking a serverless function for the first time after being idle or after a period of inactivity. When a serverless function is not actively running, it may need to be initialized, which can introduce a delay. Cold start performance can vary depending on factors like the language runtime, function complexity, and underlying infrastructure.

Scaling

Scaling in the context of serverless applications refers to the automatic adjustment of resources based on demand. In serverless computing, scaling is typically handled automatically by the platform (e.g., Azure Functions or Logic Apps), meaning the system can handle increased traffic or workload by provisioning more compute resources or adjusting capacity, and scale back when demand decreases.

Event-Driven Architecture

Event-driven architecture (EDA) is a software architecture paradigm in which the flow of program execution is determined by events. In an event-driven system, components (such as Azure Functions or Logic Apps) react to events emitted by other services or systems, making the system more decoupled and responsive. This architecture is ideal for serverless solutions, where events can trigger specific actions like running functions or triggering workflows.

Service Bus

Azure Service Bus is a fully managed message broker service in Azure that facilitates communication between different applications and services. It is especially useful in scenarios where decoupled communication is needed, such as asynchronous message passing or event-driven architecture. Service Bus supports multiple messaging patterns, including queues, topics, and subscriptions, allowing for reliable, scalable message delivery between services.

Infrastructure as Code (IaC)

Infrastructure as Code is the practice of defining and managing infrastructure using code, typically in a declarative or imperative style. In Azure, IaC can be implemented using tools such as ARM templates, Bicep, and Terraform. IaC ensures that infrastructure is provisioned, configured, and deployed in a consistent and automated manner, reducing errors and manual intervention.

Cold Start Latency

Cold start latency refers to the time it takes for a serverless function to initialize when it is invoked for the first time after being idle or after a period of inactivity. This can be a concern when real-time processing is required, as the initial request can experience a delay. Strategies such as warm-up techniques or optimizing the function's code can help reduce cold start latency.

Serverless Computing

Serverless computing refers to a cloud computing model in which developers can run applications without managing the underlying infrastructure. The cloud provider automatically handles the provisioning, scaling, and management of the infrastructure, allowing developers to focus purely on writing code. In Azure, serverless computing is primarily provided through services such as Azure Functions and Logic Apps.

Workflow Automation

Workflow automation is the process of automating complex business processes, often involving multiple steps or services, without manual intervention. Azure Logic Apps is a key tool for implementing workflow automation, enabling businesses to integrate systems and automate repetitive tasks. Workflows can be triggered by various events, such as incoming emails, database changes, or user interactions.

Monitoring and Diagnostics

Monitoring and diagnostics in the context of serverless computing refer to the tools and techniques used to observe and troubleshoot the performance of serverless applications. Azure provides services such as Azure Monitor, Application Insights, and Log Analytics to help developers and administrators monitor the health, performance, and usage of serverless applications, identify issues, and make data-driven improvements.

Cost Management

Cost management in Azure refers to the process of monitoring and optimizing spending on Azure services. For serverless applications, cost management is particularly important, as costs are based on usage (e.g., function execution time or number of invocations). Azure provides tools such as Azure Cost Management and Azure Pricing Calculator to help organizations estimate and control costs associated with serverless applications.

By understanding these key terms, you'll be better equipped to design, deploy, and manage serverless applications on Azure. These terms will also help you understand the deeper concepts discussed in the chapters that follow, enabling you to make informed decisions as you begin your serverless journey with Azure.

Resources for Further Learning

As you continue your exploration of serverless computing on Azure, it is important to build on the foundational knowledge you've gained. Azure is a vast ecosystem, and to fully take advantage of its capabilities, ongoing learning is essential. This section will guide you to additional resources, including documentation, online courses, books, and communities that will help you deepen your understanding of serverless computing, Azure services, and cloud development in general.

1. Official Azure Documentation

The first place to turn when seeking information about any Azure service is the official Microsoft Azure documentation. This documentation is comprehensive, regularly updated, and provides detailed guides on both basic and advanced topics related to Azure services. Below are some essential links and areas of focus within the Azure documentation that will help you expand your skills in serverless computing.

- **Azure Functions Documentation**
  Azure Functions allows you to run code in response to events without managing infrastructure. The documentation provides thorough guidance on setting up and configuring Azure Functions, as well as examples for various programming languages.

  - Link: Azure Functions Documentation

- **Azure Logic Apps Documentation**
  Logic Apps is another critical service for building serverless applications. The documentation here will help you understand how to design workflows, integrate services, and deploy solutions using Azure Logic Apps.

  - Link: Azure Logic Apps Documentation

- **Azure Event Grid Documentation**
  For event-driven architectures, Event Grid is a key service. It enables event routing between Azure services and external systems. The documentation will guide you on how to set up event subscriptions and handle events in a scalable, reliable manner.

  - Link: Azure Event Grid Documentation

- **Durable Functions Documentation**
  Durable Functions is an extension of Azure Functions that allows you to build stateful workflows in a serverless environment. This section of the documentation will provide insight into how to work with durable entities, timers, and activity functions.

    ○ Link: Durable Functions Documentation

2. Microsoft Learn: Interactive Learning Paths

Microsoft Learn is an online platform offering interactive tutorials, modules, and learning paths designed to help you master Azure services. It's an excellent way to gain hands-on experience and build practical skills. The learning paths are designed to take you step by step through real-world scenarios, and they cover both beginner and advanced topics.

- **Serverless Computing on Azure**
  This learning path provides a hands-on introduction to serverless development on Azure. It covers key services such as Azure Functions, Logic Apps, Event Grid, and Durable Functions, and walks you through real-world use cases. The path also includes interactive exercises, making it ideal for those who learn best by doing.

  ○ Link: Serverless Computing on Azure Learning Path

- **Azure Functions Developer Learning Path**
  This is a more focused learning path that dives deep into Azure Functions, covering topics like triggers, bindings, and best practices for deploying and monitoring functions. If you are looking to specialize in Azure Functions, this path is ideal.

  ○ Link: Azure Functions Developer Learning Path

- **Developing Solutions with Azure Logic Apps**
  Logic Apps is a powerful tool for automating workflows in a serverless environment. This learning path will guide you through using Logic Apps to connect services, build integrations, and create scalable workflows.

  ○ Link: Developing Solutions with Azure Logic Apps Learning Path

3. Online Courses and Certifications

For a more structured approach to learning, online courses and certifications can provide a roadmap to mastering Azure serverless technologies. These courses often include video lectures, quizzes, and assignments that allow you to learn at your own pace.

- **Pluralsight Azure Serverless Learning Paths**
  Pluralsight offers a comprehensive range of courses on Azure services, including serverless technologies. The courses are taught by industry experts and cover both introductory and advanced topics. You can find specific learning paths dedicated to Azure Functions, Logic Apps, and event-driven architectures.

  ○ Link: Pluralsight Azure Serverless Learning Paths

- **Udemy Courses**
  Udemy offers several courses on Azure serverless technologies, often at affordable prices. Many courses are taught by experienced developers and include real-world projects. Look for courses that cover Azure Functions, Logic Apps, and serverless architecture design.

  - Link: Udemy Azure Courses

- **Microsoft Certified: Azure Developer Associate Certification (AZ-204)**
  If you are looking for an industry-recognized certification, the AZ-204: Developing Solutions for Microsoft Azure certification is a great option. This certification exam covers various Azure development topics, including serverless computing. It is an excellent way to validate your skills and stand out in the job market.

  - Link: AZ-204 Certification

4. Books

In addition to the resources provided by Microsoft and online learning platforms, books offer a deeper, more comprehensive understanding of serverless computing and Azure. Here are a few recommended books that cover Azure serverless services and cloud development:

- **"Serverless Architectures on AWS" by Peter Sbarski**
  While focused on AWS, this book provides an excellent foundation for understanding serverless concepts, which are transferable to Azure. It dives into building and managing serverless applications and offers hands-on examples using AWS services that can easily be adapted to Azure's offerings.

- **"Microsoft Azure Serverless Computing" by Pradeep Gohil**
  This book provides an in-depth look at serverless computing on Azure, with detailed examples of using Azure Functions, Logic Apps, and other services to build scalable serverless applications. It covers architecture patterns, deployment strategies, and monitoring techniques.

- **"Cloud Native Patterns" by Cornelia Davis**
  This book covers cloud-native patterns that are applicable in a variety of cloud platforms, including Azure. It dives into patterns for building scalable, reliable, and cost-effective serverless applications, and includes guidance on design, architecture, and security.

- **"Hands-On Serverless Computing with Azure" by Saurabh Bansal**
  Focused specifically on Azure, this book walks you through building and deploying serverless applications using Azure Functions, Logic Apps, and Event Grid. It provides practical examples and best practices for leveraging Azure serverless offerings in real-world scenarios.

5. Communities and Forums

Learning from others is a vital part of growing your expertise in serverless computing. Joining communities, forums, and developer groups will help you stay up-to-date with the latest trends, get help when you're stuck, and share your knowledge with others.

- **Microsoft Developer Community**
  The Microsoft Developer Community is an excellent place to ask questions, share insights, and get help from other developers who work with Azure. You can find discussions on specific Azure services and topics related to serverless computing.

    - Link: Microsoft Developer Community

- **Stack Overflow**
  As one of the largest programming communities, Stack Overflow is an invaluable resource for developers working with Azure. You can find answers to questions on serverless computing, Azure Functions, Logic Apps, and other related topics.

    - Link: Stack Overflow - Azure

- **Azure Forums and Reddit**
  There are several forums and subreddits dedicated to Azure, including the Azure subreddit, where you can find discussions about serverless computing and ask questions about specific challenges you may be facing.

    - Link: Azure Subreddit

- **Meetups and Conferences**
  Participating in Azure-related meetups, webinars, and conferences is another great way to learn and network with other professionals in the cloud development space. Microsoft hosts events like Microsoft Ignite, and local meetups often feature sessions on serverless development.

- **Serverless Framework Community**
  The Serverless Framework is a popular open-source framework for building and deploying serverless applications. The framework's community is active, with numerous discussions on best practices and tutorials for working with serverless architectures, including on Azure.

    - Link: Serverless Framework Community

6. Blogs and Tutorials

Reading blogs and tutorials written by experts in the field can provide you with useful insights, tips, and best practices for serverless development. Here are some key blogs and resources to follow:

- **Microsoft Azure Blog**
  The official Microsoft Azure blog provides updates, news, and in-depth articles on new features and services within the Azure ecosystem. It is a reliable source for the latest announcements related to serverless technologies and best practices.

  - Link: Microsoft Azure Blog

- **Serverless.com Blog**
  This blog focuses on all things serverless and often features articles on using the Serverless Framework with Azure. It's a great place to find detailed guides, tutorials, and examples on building serverless applications.

  - Link: Serverless Blog

- **The Azure DevOps Blog**
  The Azure DevOps blog covers the latest in Azure DevOps tools, CI/CD pipelines, and best practices for deploying and managing serverless applications on Azure. It's a great resource for integrating serverless technologies with DevOps workflows.

  - Link: Azure DevOps Blog

By leveraging these resources, you can deepen your knowledge of Azure and serverless computing, keep up with industry trends, and build on the foundation provided in this book. The Azure ecosystem is constantly evolving, and continuing to learn and engage with the community will ensure that you stay ahead of the curve in the serverless space.

Sample Projects and Code Snippets

In this section, we will explore several practical examples that demonstrate the power of Azure's serverless technologies. These sample projects and code snippets will help you get hands-on experience with Azure Functions, Logic Apps, and other serverless components. By working through these examples, you will be able to gain a deeper understanding of how these services can be used to solve real-world problems. These samples will cover basic scenarios to more advanced use cases, providing a wide range of learning opportunities.

1. Azure Functions: A Simple HTTP Trigger

The simplest and most common scenario for Azure Functions is using an HTTP trigger. This example will demonstrate how to create an HTTP-triggered Azure Function that responds to requests and returns a simple message.

Steps to create an HTTP-triggered Azure Function:

1. **Create a Function App in the Azure Portal**
   In the Azure Portal, create a new Function App by selecting "Create a resource" and then choosing "Function App" under the "Compute" category. Choose your subscription, resource group, and region. Once the Function App is created, you can

deploy and manage functions inside it.

2. **Create a New Function**
   In the Function App, click on "Functions" and then select "Add" to create a new function. Choose the "HTTP trigger" template.

3. **Write the Function Code**
   Once the function is created, replace the default code with the following sample:

```csharp
using System.IO;
using Microsoft.AspNetCore.Mvc;
using Microsoft.Azure.WebJobs;
using Microsoft.Azure.WebJobs.Extensions.Http;
using Microsoft.Azure.WebJobs.Extensions.Mvc;
using Microsoft.Extensions.Logging;

public static class HelloFunction
{
    [FunctionName("HelloWorld")]
    public static async Task<IActionResult> Run(
        [HttpTrigger(AuthorizationLevel.Function, "get", "post")]
HttpRequest req,
        ILogger log)
    {
        log.LogInformation("C# HTTP trigger function processed a
request.");

        string name = req.Query["name"];

        return new OkObjectResult($"Hello, {name}");
    }
}
```

Explanation of the Code:

- **[HttpTrigger]**: This attribute binds the function to an HTTP trigger, allowing the function to be invoked by an HTTP request.

- **ILogger log**: This is used for logging information about the execution of the function.

- **HttpRequest req**: This provides access to the HTTP request that triggered the function.

- **OkObjectResult**: This is used to return a successful HTTP response with a message.

Running the Function:

Once you deploy the function, you can test it by sending an HTTP GET or POST request to the provided URL, appending a `name` query parameter. For example, you could use `curl` to test:

```
curl "https://<your-function-app-
name>.azurewebsites.net/api/HelloWorld?name=Azure"
```

This would return the response: `Hello, Azure`.

2. Logic Apps: Building a Workflow to Send Email Notifications

In this section, we'll create a Logic App that sends an email notification when a new file is uploaded to an Azure Storage Blob container. This example demonstrates the power of Logic Apps to integrate different services and automate workflows without writing code.

Steps to create the Logic App:

1. **Create a Logic App**
   In the Azure Portal, go to "Create a resource" and search for "Logic App". Create a new Logic App and choose the desired resource group and location.

2. **Design the Workflow**
   After the Logic App is created, open the designer. For this workflow, we'll use the trigger "When a blob is added or modified (properties only)" to detect when a file is uploaded to a Blob container.

3. **Configure the Trigger**
   Select the Azure Storage account and container where the files will be uploaded. The trigger will activate whenever a new file is added or an existing file is modified in this container.

4. **Add an Action to Send an Email**
   Add the action "Send an email (V2)" from the Outlook connector. Configure it with the email address to which the notification should be sent and a message indicating that a new file has been uploaded.

Logic App Workflow:

- **Trigger**: When a blob is uploaded or modified in Azure Storage.

- **Action**: Send an email notification to the designated recipient.

Example Workflow:

- Trigger: When a file is uploaded to the "Documents" container in the Azure Storage account.

- Action: Send an email with the subject "New File Uploaded" and the file name as the email body.

3. Event-Driven Architecture with Azure Functions and Event Grid

Event-driven architecture is a common design pattern for serverless applications. In this example, we'll use Azure Event Grid to trigger an Azure Function whenever a new event occurs in Azure Storage, such as a file upload.

Steps to implement the solution:

1. **Create an Event Grid Subscription**
   In the Azure Portal, create a new Event Grid subscription that listens for events in your Azure Storage account. You can choose to subscribe to all events or filter for specific events, such as "Blob Created".

2. **Create an Azure Function to Process the Event**
   Create a new Azure Function with an Event Grid trigger. This function will be invoked whenever an event is fired by the Event Grid.

3. **Function Code Example:**

```
using Microsoft.Azure.WebJobs;
using Microsoft.Azure.WebJobs.Extensions.EventGrid;
using Microsoft.Extensions.Logging;

public static class BlobEventHandler
{
    [FunctionName("BlobEventHandler")]
    public static void Run(
        [EventGridTrigger] EventGridEvent eventGridEvent,
        ILogger log)
    {
        log.LogInformation($"Received event:
{eventGridEvent.EventType}");
```

```
            log.LogInformation($"Blob URL:
{eventGridEvent.Data["url"]}");
       }
}
```

Explanation:

- **EventGridTrigger**: This attribute binds the function to an Event Grid event. The function is triggered by events fired from Event Grid.

- **EventGridEvent**: Represents the event data, including the event type and other details (such as the URL of the uploaded blob).

- **ILogger log**: Logs the event type and blob URL for debugging purposes.

4. **Testing the Setup**
   After configuring the Event Grid subscription and deploying the function, upload a file to the storage container. The function will trigger automatically, logging details of the event.

4. Durable Functions: Implementing a Long-Running Workflow

Durable Functions is ideal for scenarios where workflows involve multiple steps or need to run for an extended period. In this example, we'll create a Durable Function that processes a series of tasks in a sequence, such as retrieving data from an external API, processing the data, and saving the results.

Steps to implement a Durable Function:

1. **Create a Durable Function App**
   Follow the same steps as creating an Azure Function, but select the "Durable Function" template.

2. **Write the Orchestrator Function**
   The orchestrator function will manage the sequence of activities.

```
[FunctionName("DurableOrchestrator")]
public static async Task RunOrchestrator(
    [OrchestrationTrigger] IDurableOrchestrationContext context)
{
    var input = context.GetInput<string>();
    var result = await
context.CallActivityAsync<string>("DurableActivity", input);
    return result;
```

}

3. **Write the Activity Function**
   This activity function will perform a specific task within the workflow.

```
[FunctionName("DurableActivity")]
public static string SayHello([ActivityTrigger] string name, ILogger
log)
{
    log.LogInformation($"Saying hello to {name}");
    return $"Hello, {name}!";
}
```

4. **Calling the Orchestrator Function**
   The client function will start the orchestration.

```
[FunctionName("DurableClient")]
public static async Task RunClient(
    [HttpTrigger(AuthorizationLevel.Function, "get", "post")]
HttpRequestMessage req,
    [DurableClient] IDurableOrchestrationClient starter,
    ILogger log)
{
    string instanceId = await
starter.StartNewAsync("DurableOrchestrator", "Azure");
    return starter.CreateCheckStatusResponse(req, instanceId);
}
```

Explanation:

- **DurableOrchestrator**: This function orchestrates the workflow and calls multiple activity functions.

- **DurableActivity**: This is the activity function that performs the actual task.

- **DurableClient**: This client function triggers the orchestrator function by invoking it via HTTP.

5. Serverless CI/CD with Azure DevOps

For deploying and managing serverless applications, CI/CD pipelines are essential. This section will show how to set up a basic CI/CD pipeline for deploying an Azure Function using Azure DevOps.

Steps to create the CI/CD pipeline:

1. **Create a New Pipeline**
   In Azure DevOps, create a new pipeline and connect it to your repository (e.g., GitHub, Azure Repos).

2. **Define the Build Pipeline**
   Define the build pipeline to restore dependencies, build the function app, and package it for deployment.

```yaml
trigger:
- main

pool:
  vmImage: 'ubuntu-latest'

steps:
- task: UseDotNet@2
  inputs:
    packageType: 'sdk'
    version: '5.x'

- task: DotNetCoreCLI@2
  inputs:
    command: 'restore'
    projects: '**/*.csproj'

- task: DotNetCoreCLI@2
  inputs:
    command: 'build'
    projects: '**/*.csproj'

- task: DotNetCoreCLI@2
  inputs:
    command: 'publish'
    publishWebProjects: true
    arguments: '--configuration Release --output
$(Build.ArtifactStagingDirectory)'
```

3. **Define the Release Pipeline**
   Set up a release pipeline to deploy the function to Azure after the build is successful. You can use the Azure Functions deployment task in Azure DevOps for this purpose.

Conclusion

These sample projects and code snippets provide a wide array of practical examples for working with Azure's serverless offerings. By going through these projects, you will gain hands-on experience with Azure Functions, Logic Apps, Event Grid, Durable Functions, and Azure DevOps, all of which are key components in building serverless applications.

API Reference Guide

This section provides an in-depth API reference for Azure's serverless offerings, focusing on Azure Functions, Logic Apps, Event Grid, Durable Functions, and related services. The reference will include descriptions of commonly used methods, properties, and key components. Understanding these APIs is crucial for interacting with Azure services programmatically, building automation, and integrating different Azure components into a cohesive serverless solution.

1. Azure Functions API

Azure Functions provides a variety of triggers, bindings, and features that enable developers to create serverless applications. Below is a reference for the key aspects of the Azure Functions API.

Function Definitions

[FunctionName]
The [FunctionName] attribute is used to define the name of the function within your code. This name is used to identify the function in the Azure portal and is a required attribute for any function.

```
[FunctionName("HelloWorld")]
public static async Task
Run([HttpTrigger(AuthorizationLevel.Function, "get", "post")]
HttpRequest req, ILogger log)
{
    log.LogInformation("C# HTTP trigger function processed a
request.");
    return new OkObjectResult("Hello, world!");
}
```

•

Input and Output Bindings

Bindings allow Azure Functions to receive and send data to external sources. Bindings can be input (to pull data into the function) or output (to send data from the function).

Input Bindings
Input bindings allow you to fetch data from external sources (like databases, storage, or HTTP services). For example, a binding to a Cosmos DB:

```
[FunctionName("ProcessData")]
public static void Run(
    [CosmosDBTrigger(
        databaseName: "MyDatabase",
        collectionName: "MyCollection",
        ConnectionStringSetting = "CosmosDBConnectionString")]
IReadOnlyList<Document> documents,
    ILogger log)
{
    log.LogInformation($"Documents modified: {documents.Count}");
}
```

•

Output Bindings
Output bindings send data from the function to external systems. For example, saving data to Azure Blob Storage:

```
[FunctionName("SaveToBlob")]
public static async Task Run(
    [HttpTrigger(AuthorizationLevel.Function, "get", "post")]
HttpRequest req,
    [Blob("mycontainer/{rand-guid}", FileAccess.Write)] Stream
outputBlob,
    ILogger log)
{
    var message = "Hello, this is written to a blob!";
    using (var writer = new StreamWriter(outputBlob))
    {
        await writer.WriteAsync(message);
    }
}
```

•

Function Triggers

Triggers specify the event that causes the function to execute. Azure Functions supports various trigger types, such as HTTP requests, timers, and messages from queues.

HTTP Trigger
An HTTP trigger allows a function to respond to HTTP requests:

```
[FunctionName("HttpTriggerFunction")]
public static async Task<HttpResponseMessage>
Run([HttpTrigger(AuthorizationLevel.Function, "get", "post")]
HttpRequestMessage req, ILogger log)
{
    log.LogInformation("HTTP trigger function executed.");
    return req.CreateResponse(HttpStatusCode.OK, "Hello, Azure!");
}
```

-

Timer Trigger
A timer trigger allows you to execute a function at specified intervals:

```
[FunctionName("TimerTriggerFunction")]
public static void Run([TimerTrigger("0 */5 * * * *")] TimerInfo
timer, ILogger log)
{
    log.LogInformation($"Timer trigger executed at:
{DateTime.Now}");
}
```

-

Queue Trigger
A queue trigger listens for messages in an Azure Storage Queue:

```
[FunctionName("QueueTriggerFunction")]
public static void Run(
    [QueueTrigger("myqueue", Connection = "AzureWebJobsStorage")]
string message,
    ILogger log)
{
    log.LogInformation($"Received message: {message}");
}
```

-

2. Logic Apps API

Logic Apps offer a robust API for automating workflows between services. Below are the key components when working with Logic Apps programmatically.

Workflow Triggers

When an HTTP request is received
This trigger is used to start a Logic App when an HTTP request is sent to the endpoint:

```
{
  "definition": {
    "$schema": "https://schema.management.azure.com/schemas/2018-11-01/workflowdefinition.json#",
    "content": {
      "type": "HttpRequest",
      "method": "POST",
      "uri": "https://<your-logic-app-endpoint>"
    }
  }
}
```

-

Recurrence Trigger
A recurrence trigger runs a workflow at defined intervals, such as daily or hourly:

```
{
  "definition": {
    "$schema": "https://schema.management.azure.com/schemas/2018-11-01/workflowdefinition.json#",
    "content": {
      "type": "Recurrence",
      "frequency": "Day",
      "interval": 1
    }
  }
}
```

-

Actions

Actions define the tasks that the Logic App will perform after a trigger is invoked. For instance, to send an email with Outlook:

Send an email (V2)
This action sends an email through Outlook:

```
{
  "content": {
    "type": "SendEmail",
    "to": "recipient@example.com",
    "subject": "New Blob Uploaded",
    "body": "A new blob has been uploaded to your container."
  }
}
```

-

Error Handling

Logic Apps support error handling by using "Run After" settings. This enables workflows to take specific actions based on the success or failure of previous steps.

3. Event Grid API

Event Grid is designed to help you build event-driven architectures. Below are the key components of the Event Grid API.

Event Subscriptions
Creating an Event Subscription

To subscribe to events from a resource like an Azure Storage account, use the following API request:

```
{
  "properties": {
    "destination": {
      "endpointType": "Webhook",
      "properties": {
        "url": "https://<your-function-url>"
      }
    },
    "filter": {
      "includedEventTypes": ["Microsoft.Storage.BlobCreated"]
    }
  }
}
```

-

Publishing Events

Event Grid allows you to publish events to an endpoint via a simple HTTP POST request. Below is an example of how to send an event to an Event Grid topic:

```json
{
  "eventType": "Microsoft.Storage.BlobCreated",
  "subject":
"/blobServices/default/containers/mycontainer/blobs/myblob.txt",
  "data": {
    "url": "https://<your-storage-
account>.blob.core.windows.net/mycontainer/myblob.txt"
  },
  "eventTime": "2025-04-09T13:00:00Z",
  "id": "12345",
  "dataVersion": "1.0",
  "metadataVersion": "1"
}
```

Event Handling

Once an event is published, it will be routed to the subscribed endpoint (like an Azure Function or Logic App). The receiving service will handle the event data based on the configuration of the subscription.

4. Durable Functions API

Durable Functions extend Azure Functions to enable long-running workflows. These functions provide several key features, including orchestration, activity functions, and state persistence.

Orchestrator Functions

An orchestrator function coordinates multiple activity functions and allows you to maintain state across function calls.

Orchestrator Function Example

An orchestrator function can call multiple activity functions and handle their results:

```csharp
[FunctionName("Orchestrator")]
public static async Task<string> RunOrchestrator(
    [OrchestrationTrigger] IDurableOrchestrationContext context)
{
    var result1 = await
context.CallActivityAsync<string>("Activity1", "input1");
    var result2 = await
context.CallActivityAsync<string>("Activity2", "input2");
```

```
    return $"{result1} and {result2}";
}
```

•

Activity Functions

Activity functions perform the tasks that are part of the workflow. They are called by the orchestrator function.

Activity Function Example

An activity function can perform a specific task, such as processing data:

```
[FunctionName("Activity1")]
public static string Activity1([ActivityTrigger] string input,
ILogger log)
{
    log.LogInformation($"Processing input: {input}");
    return $"Processed {input}";
}
```

•

Client Functions

The client function is responsible for starting the orchestration by calling the orchestrator function.

Client Function Example

The client function triggers the orchestrator function and returns a status response:

```
[FunctionName("ClientFunction")]
public static async Task<HttpResponseMessage> RunClient(
    [HttpTrigger(AuthorizationLevel.Function, "get", "post")]
HttpRequestMessage req,
    [DurableClient] IDurableOrchestrationClient starter,
    ILogger log)
{
    string instanceId = await starter.StartNewAsync("Orchestrator",
null);
    return starter.CreateCheckStatusResponse(req, instanceId);
}
```

•

Conclusion

This API reference guide covers essential APIs for interacting with Azure Functions, Logic Apps, Event Grid, and Durable Functions. By understanding these APIs, you can integrate Azure's serverless capabilities into your applications and automate workflows, events, and processes efficiently. Whether you are building simple HTTP-triggered functions or complex, long-running workflows, Azure's serverless APIs provide the flexibility and scalability to meet your needs.

Frequently Asked Questions

This section answers some of the most common questions related to serverless computing on Azure, focusing on Azure Functions, Logic Apps, Event Grid, and other key services. These questions cover a variety of topics from getting started, troubleshooting, optimizing performance, to cost management. Whether you are new to Azure serverless or looking for deeper insights, these answers will help guide you in the right direction.

1. What is serverless computing, and how does it work on Azure?

Serverless computing is a cloud-native development model where developers can write and deploy code without managing or provisioning the underlying infrastructure. With serverless, you focus solely on writing the business logic of your application, and the cloud provider (Azure) takes care of managing the resources such as compute, storage, and scaling.

Azure provides several serverless services, including Azure Functions, Logic Apps, and Event Grid. These services allow developers to create event-driven applications, automate workflows, and process data in real time, all without worrying about server provisioning, scaling, or maintenance.

- **Azure Functions**: Execute small pieces of code in response to events.

- **Logic Apps**: Automate workflows between services and integrate APIs without writing code.

- **Event Grid**: Route events between Azure services, enabling event-driven architectures.

2. What are the main benefits of using Azure Functions?

Azure Functions offer several advantages for developers looking to build serverless applications. Some of the key benefits include:

- **Scalability**: Functions automatically scale up or down based on the number of incoming events, ensuring that resources are used efficiently and only when needed.

- **Cost Efficiency**: You pay only for the execution time of your functions, meaning there are no charges for idle time. This model is highly cost-effective for applications with unpredictable workloads.

- **Event-driven**: Azure Functions can be triggered by a wide range of events, including HTTP requests, queue messages, file uploads, and database changes.

- **Easy Integration**: Functions can integrate seamlessly with other Azure services, such as Azure Storage, Cosmos DB, Service Bus, and Logic Apps.

- **Supports Multiple Languages**: Azure Functions supports several programming languages, including C#, JavaScript, Python, Java, and PowerShell, allowing developers to use their preferred language.

3. How do I handle state in Azure Functions?

Azure Functions are inherently stateless, meaning each invocation is independent and does not persist state across function executions. However, there are several ways to manage state across invocations:

Durable Functions: Durable Functions, an extension of Azure Functions, enable you to create stateful workflows. You can define orchestrations, manage long-running workflows, and maintain state between different function calls.

Example: Using Durable Functions to maintain state across multiple steps:

```
[FunctionName("DurableOrchestrator")]
public static async Task<string> RunOrchestrator(
    [OrchestrationTrigger] IDurableOrchestrationContext context)
{
    var input = context.GetInput<string>();
    var result = await context.CallActivityAsync<string>("Activity1", input);
    return result;
}

[FunctionName("Activity1")]
public static string Activity1([ActivityTrigger] string input,
ILogger log)
{
    log.LogInformation($"Processing {input}");
    return $"Processed {input}";
}
```

-
- **External Storage**: If you need to store state temporarily or persist it between function calls, you can use Azure Storage (Blob Storage, Table Storage), Cosmos DB, or

other databases to store and retrieve the data.

- **In-memory Storage (Not Recommended for Long-term State)**: You can use in-memory solutions like static variables, but this approach is not recommended for long-term state persistence since the function could be scaled out, leading to different instances handling requests.

4. What is the difference between Logic Apps and Azure Functions?

While both Logic Apps and Azure Functions are part of Azure's serverless offerings, they are designed for different purposes:

- **Azure Functions**: Ideal for executing small pieces of code in response to events. Azure Functions are code-first, where you write your business logic directly.

  Example: Azure Functions are best for processing data, handling HTTP requests, and integrating with external services through APIs or event-driven triggers.

- **Logic Apps**: A workflow automation service that enables you to visually design workflows and integrate with over 200 services, including databases, APIs, and SaaS applications. Logic Apps are designed for building complex workflows with minimal code.

  Example: Logic Apps are great for automating tasks like sending emails, updating databases, or connecting various systems without writing code. For example, a Logic App can send an email notification when a file is uploaded to a storage account.

In summary, use Azure Functions when you need fine-grained control over the execution of code, and use Logic Apps when you want to automate workflows between different services with a low-code/no-code approach.

5. How does Azure Event Grid work with serverless applications?

Azure Event Grid enables event-driven architectures by routing events from various sources to different subscribers, including Azure Functions, Logic Apps, and Webhooks. Event Grid is ideal for triggering workflows and serverless functions in response to events like file uploads, database changes, or custom events.

- **Event Sources**: Azure services like Azure Storage, Resource Groups, or even custom events from your application.

- **Event Handlers**: Azure Functions, Logic Apps, or external endpoints that process the events.

Example of using Azure Event Grid to trigger a function when a file is uploaded to Azure Blob Storage:

```
{
  "eventType": "Microsoft.Storage.BlobCreated",
  "subject":
"/blobServices/default/containers/mycontainer/blobs/myblob.txt",
  "data": {
    "url": "https://<your-storage-
account>.blob.core.windows.net/mycontainer/myblob.txt"
  },
  "eventTime": "2025-04-09T13:00:00Z",
  "id": "12345",
  "dataVersion": "1.0",
  "metadataVersion": "1"
}
```

This event can be routed to an Azure Function that processes the file upload, extracts information, or triggers additional workflows.

6. What are the best practices for optimizing performance in Azure Functions?

There are several ways to optimize the performance of your Azure Functions, ensuring they run efficiently and at scale:

- **Reduce Cold Start Latency**: Cold start happens when a function is invoked after being idle for some time. To minimize cold start latency:

  - Use the **Premium Plan** or **Dedicated Plan** to ensure that your functions are always warm.

  - Use **Warm-Up Triggers** to periodically invoke functions and keep them active.

  - Optimize function code to minimize the initialization time.

- **Use Efficient Bindings**: Azure Functions support multiple input and output bindings. Ensure that you're using the most efficient binding for your use case. For example, using direct bindings to Blob Storage or Cosmos DB can be faster than making HTTP calls within your function.

- **Minimize Dependencies**: Reduce the number of external dependencies in your functions to improve startup time and minimize cold start overhead. Only include the libraries and packages that are strictly necessary.

- **Concurrency and Parallelism**: Azure Functions automatically scale based on the number of incoming events. However, you should design your functions to handle multiple concurrent executions efficiently. Use **async/await** and parallel processing techniques to ensure that the function processes requests concurrently.

7. How is cost calculated for serverless applications on Azure?

Cost for serverless services like Azure Functions, Logic Apps, and Event Grid is based on the usage of the service, including the number of executions, the duration of the function execution, and the resources consumed.

- **Azure Functions**: You are charged based on the number of function executions and the duration of each execution. The duration is calculated from the time your code starts executing to the time it finishes. You are only billed for the execution time, with the first 1 million executions per month being free.

- **Logic Apps**: Pricing for Logic Apps is based on the number of actions and triggers in your workflow. Each step in the workflow, such as sending an email or calling an API, counts as an action.

- **Event Grid**: Event Grid charges based on the number of events delivered. You are billed for the number of events published and delivered to subscribers. The first 100,000 events per month are free.

8. Can I integrate Azure Functions with other services outside of Azure?

Yes, Azure Functions can integrate with both Azure services and external services. Azure Functions can be triggered by HTTP requests, allowing integration with any service that can make HTTP calls. You can also integrate with external APIs, databases, and systems using SDKs, HTTP requests, or custom bindings.

For example, to call an external REST API within an Azure Function:

```
using System.Net.Http;

[FunctionName("CallExternalApi")]
public static async Task Run([TimerTrigger("0 */5 * * * *")]
TimerInfo myTimer, ILogger log)
{
    using (HttpClient client = new HttpClient())
    {
        var response = await
client.GetAsync("https://api.example.com/data");
```

```
        var data = await response.Content.ReadAsStringAsync();
        log.LogInformation($"API Response: {data}");
    }
}
```

Azure Functions also support bindings for third-party services, such as sending data to Salesforce or Slack, and you can create custom bindings for additional integrations.

9. What are the common challenges when using serverless computing on Azure?

While serverless computing offers many advantages, there are some challenges that developers may face:

- **Cold Start**: As mentioned earlier, functions may experience a delay when invoked after a period of inactivity. This can impact latency-sensitive applications. However, choosing a premium plan or implementing warm-up strategies can help mitigate this.

- **State Management**: Azure Functions are stateless by design, which can be challenging when workflows require maintaining state across multiple executions. Durable Functions can help address this challenge, but they may require a learning curve.

- **Debugging and Monitoring**: Debugging serverless applications can be more challenging due to the lack of local execution environments and the distributed nature of serverless workloads. Tools like Application Insights can help monitor and diagnose issues, but there may still be complexities when working with large-scale systems.

- **Vendor Lock-in**: Serverless applications often rely on proprietary services provided by cloud providers. This can lead to vendor lock-in, making it more difficult to move to other platforms in the future.

10. How can I test and debug serverless applications?

Testing and debugging serverless applications can be tricky due to their stateless and event-driven nature. However, there are strategies and tools that can help:

- **Local Development**: Azure Functions provides tools for local development, such as the Azure Functions Core Tools, which allow you to run and test functions on your local machine before deploying them to Azure.

- **Unit Testing**: For Azure Functions, you can use frameworks like MSTest or xUnit to write unit tests for your functions. Mocking dependencies and using dependency injection can make it easier to isolate your functions for testing.

- **Application Insights**: Use Application Insights to collect telemetry data and logs from your serverless application. This will help you monitor performance, track errors, and troubleshoot issues.

By answering these frequently asked questions, this section aims to provide clarity on key concepts and challenges related to Azure serverless computing. As you continue to work with Azure's serverless offerings, keep these answers in mind to help you design, deploy, and manage efficient serverless applications.